The Eye of the Storm

Centered in Christ

Wendy C. Collins

The Eye of the Storm

Centered in Christ
Wendy C. Collins

Editing - Norma Ludy
Layout & Design - Gary Collins
Cover Photo - Dreamstime.com

All rights reserved.
© 2008
Gary C. Collins Publishing

No part of this book may be reproduced or transmitted in any form or by any means, electronic or mechanical, including photocopying, recording, or by any information storage and retrieval system for any other reason.

Quality Speech Materials
Box 955
Fountain Inn, SC 29644

www.QualitySpeech.com
864-862-7640

Leader's Book

A leader's book that goes with this text is available. It can be used for group ladies Bibles studies. You can obtain one online or by phone from:

www.QualitySpeech.com
864-862-7640

Table Of Contents

1 - THE STORM OF LIFE — — — — — — — — — — — — — 1

2 - PRELUDE TO THE STORM — — — — — — — — — — 21

3 - TRUST IN THE STORM — — — — — — — — — — — 43

4 - COURAGE IN THE STORM — — — — — — — — — — 63

5 - PEACE IN THE STORM — — — — — — — — — — — 81

6 - JOY IN THE STORM — — — — — — — — — — — — 109

7 - SAFE IN THE STORM — — — — — — — — — — — — 125

8 - COMFORT IN THE STORM — — — — — — — — — — 137

9 - THE PASSING OF THE STORM — — — — — — — — 155

10 - THE VALUE OF THE STORM — — — — — — — — — 173

To Rynda and Stephen
who found
Sunshine after the Storm.

The Storm of Life

THE EYE OF THE STORM

When I was a teenager, every summer my mom, dad, and I would pack up our clothes and move to our little cottage on a lake in the Irish Hills of Michigan. It was about 40 miles from home and Dad drove back and forth from there to work every day.

It wasn't a fancy cottage. Just a simple cabin that my grandpa and dad had constructed shortly after World War II. It wasn't winterized. There was no insulation. No furnace either. In fact, for years there was no shower. We just took a bar of soap down to the lake each night to use during our evening swim.

There was no basement in the cottage, which was not a good thing in that area of Michigan which was nicknamed "Tornado Alley." Quite often during the summer months the weatherman would warn us of a tornado watch and we had no place of safety in which we could hide.

The lack of a basement at our cottage was a fact that tortured my mother to no end. She worried about it often. When the weatherman announced a tornado warning or watch for our area, Mom would jump up to look out of the cottage windows. She would run around gathering the things she wanted to make sure didn't blow away and would pile them together. I can still hear her fretting and stewing about the fact that we had no basement to keep us safe and we didn't know anyone who did. We had nowhere to go to hide. She would wish aloud that we were back home where we had a basement and we could be safe!

The Eye of the Storm

How often in life, when one of life's storms hit, do we feel like we have nowhere to go, nowhere to hide? We run around, so to speak, trying to find a safe place. But we can see none. Our hearts are filled with fear and downright panic. We begin to fret and stew.

A tornado never actually touched down in our area in all the summers we spent at the lake, but one year I experienced something very strange. The TV weatherman was warning of a possible tornado heading our way. My mother began her usual pre-tornado panic fest. I, on the other hand, since I knew there was nowhere to go anyway, decided to go outside to watch the sky to see if I could spot a tornado coming.

In the distance it looked like some very nasty weather was heading our way. The sky was filled with clouds that were an inky gray color and they rolled toward me in a strange way. The wind whipped furiously around me. The rain began to come down in droves. I could barely see. This was no ordinary storm.

Then I noticed something unusual. High above me the clouds began to swirl in somewhat of a tornado-shaped funnel. They were coming directly at me, but they were not even close to making contact with the earth. The storm was so high above me that I could look up at it as it began to pass overhead, yet no damage was being done to the earth below.

All of a sudden, amidst the horrible wind and rain, there came an abrupt calm. For a moment the sun was shining. The wind and rain stopped. It was completely quiet and peaceful. It was an astounding and uncanny transformation.

Then, just as suddenly, the clouds rolled back in and darkened the skies once more. The wind and rain picked up at a terrible rate, and the storm continued on over and beyond me. I watched as it went on its way.

It dawned on me that for one short moment I had been in the eye of the storm, and all was peace and quiet.

Storms will come in life. No one can escape that inevitable fact. But even though the storm rages all around you, you can be safe in the eye of the storm. You can be safe hidden in the center of God's will for your life.

I found out in my storm, there is a safe place! It is hidden in God.

If you allow it, each storm you face can be molding and shaping your life so that day by day you are becoming more and more like your perfect example, Jesus Christ.

My Storm

I want to begin by telling you that I am not a Christian Psychologist or a Counselor of any type. I don't have all the answers. I don't even have all the questions.

I have not experienced every type of trouble and grief that can be faced. But I have faced a few hard times. I am not an expert on trials or troubles. I have just had my share of them and through the storms that God has allowed in my life, He has taught me some very valuable lessons.

I have been a mother, an Evangelist's wife, and a writer for many years. I would like to share some of the trials and griefs I have faced. More importantly, I would like to share how God helped me get through them day by day with the help of His Word.

I do not think that I have all the answers just because I have been in the ministry or for any other reason. I have not necessarily gone through what you are going through. My trials, troubles, and griefs may not be the same as yours. My manner of handling them may not be the same. What is the same, however, is this: If you have accepted Jesus Christ as your Savior, then we share the same Grief Counselor. And He uses the same Word to give help and apply healing.

While I may not have all the answers, fortunately, I do believe that God has all the answers and they can be found in His Word. He is so kind and merciful to share those answers with us. We just need to seek His face, His answers, His way, and His timing.

We all face problems, and our problems don't have to be life-threatening to be overwhelming and troublesome. Whether you face cancer or a workplace conflict, your problems are real. They are frustrating, or fearful, or just plain depressing. They can seem unsolvable.

I have searched for ways to face the trials and griefs that have come my way. Some storms in life have been harder than others. Some have come to happy endings, some have not seemed to come to such happy endings. Or at least not the endings I would have chosen.

There have been times I have stood in life's storms and glared in anger at the dark clouds that hovered overhead. I have hunkered down in fear as the lightening flashed and the thunder roared. And I have bowed my head with grief in the driving rain.

But through every hard time I have faced, I can truthfully say, God has always been good and faithful to me. God has never let me down. And

God's way has always proven best. God deserves glory for all His ways.

To be very honest, I am writing this as a way to work through one of the hardest storms that I have ever had to face: the death of my son-in-law, Bo. Writing is my way of letting go and moving on. Over the years I have found that writing is a special gift God has given to help me work out life's problems. Hopefully, as I work things out, so will you.

Most of this story is from my perspective and that is a very limited perspective. Actually, most of what my son-in-law and daughter, Rynda, went through was much more intense then anything I experienced during the same time. It would be self-centered for me to suggest that what I went through was as bad or worse than what Bo and Rynda did, but I can't write about how they felt. I only know me and what I saw and felt.

My daughter has, thankfully, moved on. I didn't ask her to rehash her old feelings, I only asked for her permission to write about this storm. So I will just say, this is "Mom's point of view."

At the same time my son-in-law was fighting cancer, my mother was also quite sick. She was elderly and approaching the end of her life. Watching my mother become sicker and weaker was a totally different type of heartache and loss, but a very real one also.

There was a point when it felt like I had grief piled on grief. It was everywhere I turned. The joy in life I had known was gone. I wondered if it would ever be possible for me to feel joy again.

And just so you don't think that my life has been one trial or grief after another, let me add that God has kindly given me so many blessings and joys in life. God has been extremely good to me. In some ways, I feel I have been blessed with more joy than many people I have known.

But the focus of this book is life's storms and I want to be honest with you about the storm periods in my life. They have not been easy. I have had periods of deep sorrow, times of heart-searching questions for both myself and God, and moments of great fear.

I sometimes think Christians feel the need to sugar-coat their problems and their grief. Perhaps it is because they are afraid they will not seem spiritual to others if they admit to such human qualities. Heaven forbid that a Christian should be anything less than perfect in their response to life's problems!

So at the risk of someone reading this and saying, "Boy, she sure isn't very godly!" I am going to be brutally honest about my hard times and not worry about what anyone thinks. You will read things here that

I wasn't even honest enough to admit to myself until I began to work on this book. But I don't want to be guilty of sugar-coating my storms. What good would that do either one of us?

So here it is, my soul is bared to you. I hope that the life raft I clung to in my time of storm will be something you can grab onto also.

LIFE'S STORMS

The old saying goes that there are only two certainties in life: taxes and death. I would like to submit a third: storms. You can be sure that if you are not currently going through a storm, you will eventually. In fact, you will probably face many storms in your lifetime.

You never know, from moment to moment, when a storm will hit. Life is full of storms. Life is full of changes. Full of surprises. And the older you get, the more you realize that not all surprises are good. There were days when I wished the surprises would end. I prayed for a boring day!

Some problems and trials are small and some are big. Usually, at the time of a storm, all storms feel pretty big, especially if we don't have the answer to our problem. The problems I plan to address in this book are the ones that seem big to you. The ones that have no foreseeable answers.

Storms can be financial, emotional, physical, or spiritual. They can be a bothersome nuisance or a major upheaval in your life. Other people may not view your storms as all that bad, but to you they are major.

We face some storms in life much more bravely than others. We are all made of different stuff. Some of us can face a financial crisis more easily than a physical or emotional one. We all have different things that frighten and frustrate us.

A man by the name of George MacDonald once said, "Everything difficult indicates something more than our theory of life yet embraces." That is often true. Once we have faced a trial and come up with some answers, then things don't always seem so bad.

But not all storms can be overcome or solved by having the answers. And we seem to want answers. I know I prefer to know the answers. It makes me feel like I am somewhat in control. I used to want to be completely in control, but then I got so I would settle for somewhat in control. But so often, any form of control is elusive.

Slowly I discovered that I didn't need to have all the answers. I didn't need to always understand. I didn't need to solve everything. What I did need was someone to go through the storm with me. I needed someone who loved me in spite of my questions and worries. I needed someone who cared about my troubles when the rest of the world just kept going along as if nothing had happened. I needed someone to understand when no one else seemed to understand.

The good news is, I found that someone. He was there all along. That someone was God.

WHAT IS A STORM?

I define a storm as any type of upset that challenges us in a perplexing way, that troubles our heart, or that causes us frustration, pain or grief. A storm generally troubles our heart and soul. It causes us unrest and often destroys our peace of mind. Sometimes it destroys even more than that.

Some storms leave us feeling helpless and damaged. But even though a storm can leave devastation in its path, we do not need to be destroyed by the storms in our lives because we have an all powerful God who is always with us to help us through every storm. There isn't a single storm in life that we need to face alone.

II Corinthians 4:6-10 says, *For God, who commanded the light to shine out of darkness, hath shined in our hearts, to give the light of the knowledge of the glory of God in the face of Jesus Christ.*

But we have this treasure in earthen vessels, that the excellency of the power may be of God, and not of us.

We are troubled on every side, yet not distressed; we are perplexed, but not in despair;

Persecuted, but not forsaken; cast down, but not destroyed;

Always bearing about in the body the dying of the Lord Jesus, that the life also of Jesus might be made manifest in our body.

As I read that portion of Scripture, I realize God is saying that I am just a weak, clay vessel, but God places within me the priceless treasure of His salvation and grace. He does that so when others look at my life and see the storms I have weathered they will know that I could not have possibly withstood those storms by my own strength. Instead, the glory goes to God who helps me despite the storms that rage around me.

My clay pot may be bumped and kicked around and cast aside, but it has no lasting negative effect. Why? So that God will get the glory. So others will see what a difference Jesus Christ makes in my life. So others will see Christ in me.

Storms will come in life. Life is full of storms. No one can escape that inevitable fact. No one is exempt. Not even Christians. But nothing takes God by surprise. Nothing can be allowed in your life without God's permission. So even though the storm rages all around you, you can be safe in the eye of the storm. You can be safe hidden in the center of God's will for your life.

God's View Of You

I think that a couple of the most important questions everyone needs to settle in order to help them successfully weather life's storms are: "Who is God?" and "What role will God play in my life?" In other words, what is your view of God? The way you view God has a lot to do with your approach to the storms in your life.

But before we deal with your view of God, let me ask you, what is God's view of you?

In God's eyes, everyone fits into one of two categories. You are either forgiven and heading for Heaven because Jesus paid the price for your sin, or you are not forgiven and you are heading for an eternity lost and separated from God. You will pay for your own sin.

It doesn't matter to God how young or old you are, how rich or poor you are, how important or unimportant you are. God is looking at your heart's condition. You either have a heart that is filled with sin, or you have a heart that is right with Him.

You can never look into anyone else's heart. You can only look at your own heart. And an honest look at your own heart will confirm that you are sinful and painfully lacking your own goodness.

You may try, but you can never do enough good works to take away your own sinful condition. There is only one way to have a heart that is right with God. That one way is to tell God that you know you are a sinner and that you are truly sorry for your sin.

It's that simple. When you plead for God's mercy, He freely gives it. He longs to forgive and make you His child.

If you haven't settled your heart condition, right now would be a great time. The rest of this book won't do you much good if God is not your Lord and Savior. If He is not the one to whom you turn in your time of storm, then you are alone and headed for destruction. But it doesn't have to be that way.

A Right View Of God

Hopefully you have had your sin forgiven and God views you as His precious child. So the question remains, "What is your view of God?"

Even Christians often have a faulty view of God. We don't always understand God. We don't know who God really is.

Fortunately for us, God chose to give us a very candid view of who He is and what He is like when He gave us the Bible. There is no other way that we could ever know anything about God except that He so mercifully and so honestly tells us about Himself. He says, "Here I am. Get to know Me!" Then, when we do get to know God, we begin to see and understand life's storms from a more godly perspective.

God starts in Genesis by telling us He is the Creator. He tells us of how He chose a people to be special and set aside for Him. He tells of how He dealt with those people both when they obeyed and when they disobeyed.

By reading the books of Genesis through Joshua, we see that God is very much like a Father. He was a Father to the Children of Israel. They looked to Him for protection and deliverance when they were in slavery. They whined to Him when they felt all their needs were not being met. And finally, when God had led them safely into the promised land, they promptly forgot all about Him and directly disobeyed Him. They constantly rebelled, at least until they wanted another favor from Him.

God's dealings with the Children of Israel are fascinating. We heard all the Bible stories as children, but so much was skimmed over to make for more exciting stories to tell to children. It is fascinating to take a good commentary and the Bible and study the first six books of the Bible in depth. Next time you find your head above water, you may want to do that.

Moving on to the New Testament, we see how God, in reaction to Israel's rejection, throws open His arms, welcoming all who will accept

Him. We Christians have been accepted into that special group who have experienced God's deliverance from the slavery of sin.

Sometimes, like the Israelites, we also view God as a Father. And rightly so. The Bible calls God our Heavenly Father. And our Heavenly Father is often perceived to be just like our earthly father. That can be good news and bad news.

What was your father like?

My dad is a gentle, kind, and patient man. He is extremely easygoing. Mom was the disciplinarian in our family. In all my years, I have never once heard my father yell or get truly angry. I tend to see God in the same way. I really have a hard time picturing God, as He sometimes shows Himself in the Old Testament, as a Father who severely chastens His erring children when they sin.

On the other hand, I have friends that had a much harsher, judgemental father. They have no problem seeing God as the rule keeper who metes out punishment. Those friends have a difficult time seeing God as a kind and loving Father.

But God does not have the human tendencies that our earthly fathers have. He is our Father, but He is the perfect Father who neither leans too far to one side nor the other. He is perfectly just and holy while at the same time being perfectly loving and merciful.

Even so, our perspective of our Heavenly Father can be terribly distorted. And our perspective of God greatly colors our view of the storms that God allows into our lives.

We can wonder why a Father who loves us would allow such a thing to happen. Why isn't He there to stop or buffer every wind of adversity? Or we can feel that every storm is a punishment for some sin we have committed. Certainly, we may think, troubles signify that God is displeased with us!

The truth is, neither view may be correct. Only God knows the reason and purpose for each storm He allows.

Since that is the case, it is best to take a good look at God from what He says about Himself in the Scripture. Lay aside your view of your earthly father for a few minutes and instead take a closer look at just a few of the character traits of your Heavenly Father.

The Bible says God has many character traits that show His kinder, gentler side. The Bible also says God has some character traits that are sterner and certainly more difficult for us to obtain, but these attributes are not unobtainable.

God is love.

You can't even begin to imagine how much God loves you. Nothing in the world can separate you from God's love and nothing in the world could ever make God not love you. He loves you with a perfect love.

1 John 4:16 says, *And we have known and believed the love that God hath to us. God is love; and he that dwelleth in love dwelleth in God, and God in him.*

God is forgiving, merciful, and kind.

There is nothing so bad that you can do that God cannot forgive. God looks on you in mercy and waits for you to call to Him for help. God's love is directed at you. He is quick to forgive you. No matter what life may throw at you, God is always good to you.

Psalm 86:5 says, *For thou, Lord, art good, and ready to forgive; and plenteous in mercy unto all them that call upon thee.*

Luke 6:35 says, *But love ye your enemies, and do good, and lend, hoping for nothing again; and your reward shall be great, and ye shall be the children of the Highest: for he is kind unto the unthankful and to the evil.*

God is patient.

The Bible uses the word longsuffering. That's exactly what it must be like to put up with humans for God. He must suffer for a very long time as He looks down and sees how weak and foolish and sinful we humans can be. But still, He patiently deals with us.

Psalm 86:15 says, *But thou, O Lord, art a God full of compassion, and gracious, longsuffering, and plenteous in mercy and truth.*

God is faithful.

When God makes a promise to you, He keeps it. You may break many promises to Him in your lifetime, but He will never break a promise to you. He is faithful to always do what He says He will do. He is always faithful to love you.

Deuteronomy 7:9 says, *Know therefore that the LORD thy God, he is God, the faithful God, which keepeth covenant and mercy with them that love him and keep his commandments to a thousand generations.*

The Storms of Life

God is holy, righteous, and pure.

We should stand in awe of God's holiness, righteousness, and purity. We should also strive to make those qualities a part of our life. These are qualities that make us more like Christ.

1 Samuel 2:2 says, *There is none holy as the LORD: for there is none beside thee: neither is there any rock like our God.*

Psalm 119:137 says, *Righteous art thou, O LORD, and upright are thy judgments.*

Proverbs 30:5 says, *Every word of God is pure: he is a shield unto them that put their trust in him.*

God chastises His children in love.

If you are a parent, then you know that while you would love to always show your kinder, gentler side, there are moments when you must chastise and demand obedience. Not because you want to boss your children around and make them into little robots, but because you love them and want to help them to develop into responsible, God-honoring adults. You correct them in love to bring them back to the way they ought to follow. Your desire is to help them to talk, act, and think in a manner that is pleasing to both you and God.

God is the same. He chastises us to bring us to the place where we can be in close fellowship with Him and of the best service to Him. He exercises His character traits in our lives at the precise time that we need each trait. When we need patience, He is patient. When we need some righteous correction, He exercises that trait. Not to harm us, but to benefit us.

Jeremiah 30:11 says, *For I am with thee, saith the LORD, to save thee: though I make a full end of all nations whither I have scattered thee, yet will I not make a full end of thee: but I will correct thee in measure, and will not leave thee altogether unpunished.*

God allows storms, and at times, even sends storms for your good and His glory. When you react to your storm in a manner that does not please God, in a way that goes against your good and against His glory, then He must, as any good father would do, correct you. If you do not avoid sin, if you do not wait on Him, if you are not honest with Him, then He must do something that will cause you to conform to His will.

I believe God chastises in love, not in fury.

There is a difference between Biblical punishment and chastisement.

We often use the terms interchangeably but I feel that God punishes the unrighteous for their unrighteousness. He is angry with the wicked and they pay for their wickedness. Punishment falls on the sinful man.

I believe God chastises His children for an entirely different reason. God chastises those He loves to bring them back into a loving and close relationship with Him. He scolds and corrects so that you will reject your sinful ways and get things right with Him. He does it in love, not anger or revenge.

God does not punish the sin of a Christian.

That may seem like a bold statement, but it is true. Jesus took the punishment for all your sin on Himself when He died on the cross. A Christian's sin has been totally forgiven. It is covered by the blood. When you stand before God, because of the work and intercession of Jesus Christ, He sees you as pure and righteous.

However, you still sin. You have not reached sinless perfection. And your sin separates you from fellowship with God. It keeps you from being close to your sinless Father. So God has to chastise in order to restore fellowship. God chastises you to bring you into a right relationship. He loves you too much to let you go on your way, blindly moving farther and farther from the center of His will for your life. He chastises in love to bring you back.

Proverbs 3:12 says, *For whom the LORD loveth he correcteth; even as a father the son in whom he delighteth.*

Such love! Not always appreciated, but such great love, regardless.

GOD'S VIEW OF YOUR STORMS

God has a clear view of the storms that come into your life. A view you do not share. He sees the storm approaching. He watches as you seek shelter. He can look beyond and see the end of the storm.

But God does more than just watch your storm. He doesn't sit in Heaven just viewing all that transacts. He is both allowing and causing all that happens. God is in complete control. He has all power. He created the world and He sustains it. He created you and He sustains you. Without Him, you would not exist or thrive.

If you can step back from your storm long enough to take a long look at God, then you will see that all the qualities we talked about above should allow you to take a deep breath and relax. Even in your trials and troubles. You should be able to say, "Because God is loving, merciful, kind, forgiving, patient, faithful, holy, righteous, and pure, then I can trust Him completely. Even in my storm."

You can also make that statement because God is three other things that we did not discuss: God is all-knowing, all-present, and all-powerful. Those three qualities absolutely assure you that God is with you in your storm, He knows all the "what's" and "why's" of your storm, and He has the power to make everything come about that He intends. You can trust God to control your storm in such a way that it will bring good to you and glory to Him.

Even if you must weather a storm. Even if the outcome is not one you would choose. Even if you don't understand a thing about your storm. The fact that God is in control can release you from fear and frustration. It can allow you to look at your storm from a godly perspective and say, "No, I don't enjoy this storm, but I know God is in control. He is with me. He can see what I can't see. He knows what is best. He has the power to bring about what He intends. And I know He always intends for the best to happen. I can trust Him."

In His Image

All of God's character traits are good. All of His traits are traits you should diligently work to incorporate into your life.

Why? Simple. So that you can become more and more like Him. If you can be more like your Father, then when life's storms come up, you will have a better grasp on how you should handle each storm. A well-rounded view of God, a Scriptural view of God, helps you to understand how He wants you to approach the storms that He allows in your life.

You see, every trait that God has in His character is a trait He longs for you to have in your character. Some of those traits may come easily to you. Others are more evasive. But it is well worth the effort to daily work at thinking and acting more like your Heavenly Father.

I think one important reason and purpose for the storms you experience may be to cultivate His character traits in you. Storms may be allowed by God so He can make you more and more like Him. A storm may point out a trait you need and nudge you toward making that trait a part of your life.

This is an amazing thought. It is an important fact. It is one that can give hope and purpose to your storm. God may be allowing your storm in order to conform you to the image of Christ.

I write materials for Children's church. I would like to share one of the fictional stories I wrote for the children. It is based on a sermon illustration that I expanded. It is called, *In His Image*.

Once upon a time in a far away kingdom, there lived a young prince. This prince was very, very unhappy. Why was he unhappy you ask? Well, I shall tell you.

This prince seemed to have everything that anyone could want to make him happy. He had many valuable and beautiful possessions for he had been born into one of the richest kingdoms in the land. He lived in a beautiful palace. His kingdom was known and envied throughout the world for it's wealth and power and beauty.

The prince had a father, a kind and powerful king, who loved his son very much. The king wanted his son to develop into a wise and good ruler, just as he was.

One day the king decided to hire the most skilled artists in the kingdom to fashion a statue that looked exactly like he pictured his son would look when the prince would one day come to full maturity and rule in the kingdom.

The workers took great care to make sure the statue looked exactly like the prince. It wore carved robes and a crown exactly like the prince's. But there was one difference, for the statue stood straight and tall. You see, the prince, though born rich and handsome, was terribly crippled. His back was hunched over and he could never stand up straight and tall. This was why the prince was so unhappy.

But when the king pictured his son, he saw only a handsome young prince who stood erect and tall. He saw only the best in his son.

After the statue was erected and revealed to the crowd of people, the prince hung his head in shame and fled to the palace to hide.

Early the next morning, before anyone had stirred from their beds, the young prince slowly made his way out to stand before the statue. Painfully he twisted his head around to look as far up as he could. He stared up a long time at the statue. How he wished he could measure up to what his father desired him to be.

Just then a strange thought came to the prince.

The Storms of Life

"What if I stretch and stretch until eventually I can pull myself up to stand like the statue?"

So the prince stretched and stretched and stretched. He lifted his bent-over back just an inch before the poor muscles in his back refused to go any further. Then he relaxed back into place.

It hadn't worked, but the prince headed back into the palace with a smile on his face, for he had a plan.

Daily the prince would come to the statue early in the morning before anyone else in the kingdom was about. The prince would walk to the image and pull himself up as far as he could. Slowly, day by day, he found he could raise himself up an inch, then another, then another. He was making progress. But he would always retreat to the castle before anyone could see him. He never told anyone his secret.

Finally, the day came when all the kingdom was called to the palace. No one knew why they had been summoned, but everyone came and stared in great curiosity.

The king came before the people and motioned for silence. Everyone gave a great gasp and watched in awe as they viewed what seemed to be a miracle, for out of the palace walked the young prince. He stood straight and tall. He stood next to the statue and he was the exact image of it.

There was great rejoicing in the kingdom that day.

This change had not occurred overnight. Day by day, the prince had stretched his body until the muscles in his back had grown stronger and stronger. A little at a time, the prince was able to pull upright. Little by little, he became conformed to the image of the statue.

That's what God the Father, our King, wants from those who are His children. When you asked Jesus Christ to forgive your sin, you became a child of the King. But just being a child of the King does not mean that you always look and act like God, does it?

Even Christians sin. But God wants us to be in the exact image of Himself. He created us to be in His image. The Bible says in Romans 8:29 that we are to *be conformed to the image of his son.*

How can we look more and more like Jesus Christ everyday? How can we look like the image of God? Much the same way that the Prince conformed to the image of the statue. We can become conformed to Christ's image by allowing the Holy Spirit to control our lives on a daily basis.

Daily we need to ask God to help us to say the things Jesus would say when we talk to others. Daily we need to ask God to help us to do the things Jesus would do in every situation. We need to stretch our hearts and minds to be more like Him.

God has a purpose for each storm that you will ever face. And each storm, if you let it, can cause you to become more and more Christ-like. It takes effort. It takes obedience to God. Daily we need to stretch our Spiritual muscles to help us look and act more like Jesus Christ, until we are conformed to His image.

The Bible says that because of what Jesus Christ did for us on the cross, as we stand before God, He views us as perfect. He does not see our sin. He sees the blood of Jesus that completely takes away our sin. We stand upright and spotless before Him, as sinless and perfect sons and daughters of God.

While we know that here on earth we are not sinless, that is the way God views us through Christ. That is all the more reason why we should long to allow the Holy Spirit to work in our lives to help us to constantly be conforming to His image.

But God never forces us to conform to His image. Instead He gives us a choice.

We can look at the ideal set before us in God's Word and think that we can never achieve it. Or we can allow the experiences in our life to cause us to become more Christ-like. The frustrations and sorrows and suffering we face can be used of God to achieve that purpose. They can be our way of stretching our spiritual muscles into conformity.

That helps me. It may not make me FEEL better while all I seem to be experiencing is pain and sorrow, but it helps me to KNOW that there is a reason and purpose to all this pain and sorrow. It lets me know that there is value and purpose in the storms I weather. It encourages me to strap on a life jacket, batten down the hatches, and face the storm with trust in Jesus Christ. Then finally, when the storm calms and I turn my face heavenward, the Captain of my soul will smile at me and say, "You look familiar. You remind Me of My Son."

> "Oh to be like Thee! Oh to be like Thee,
> Blessed Redeemer, pure as thou art!
> Come in thy sweetness, Come in thy fullness;
> Stamp thine own image deep on my heart."
>
> *O To Be Like Thee* by Thomas Chisholm

WHAT ROLE DOES GOD PLAY?

Each storm in life is allowed to cause us to become more Christ-like. If we can get a grip on that fact, then it can greatly change the way we face our storms. It can change the way we feel about our storms and it can change the end value of our storms, not necessarily the outcome of the storm, but the outcome of the impact that it has on our life and the lives of those around us.

So, "Who is God?" God is our Father, our perfect, loving Father. And we should want to be just like Him.

The next big question is: "What role will God play in my life?"

We all react differently to God when storms come up. We may even react differently according to what type of storm we face. Here are some of the roles we allow God to play in our storms.

We get angry at God.

Often, when storms arise, the first thing we do is shake our fist at God. We get angry with God and blame Him for our problems. Therefore God plays the role of the bad guy.

We are often tempted to blame someone, anyone, for the problems in our lives. I'm not sure why blame must be assigned, but it seems to be a natural reaction. And God is easy to blame since it seems to us that if God really loved us and if He was really in control, then He would never have allowed this storm to enter our lives in the first place. God is the bad guy for allowing the storm and for not controlling it.

We ignore God.

When we ignore God, He is not allowed to play any role in our lives.

We shut God out. We decide to handle our own problems. We lay awake at night trying to think up our own solutions. We do our best to implement those solutions during the daylight. Then we lay awake again wondering if we did the right thing.

We go to everyone but God for help. We consult the experts. We call friends. We pour our income and efforts into finding help. We assume that everyone except God has the answers we are seeking.

We get out of the Word and neglect prayer. We feel all alone and it doesn't seem like God is listening anyway.

We turn to God.
When we turn to God in faith, He plays the starring role.

We can give God control of our life and our storm. When we place God in first place, we look to Him to be our strength, our peace, our joy, our comfort, our courage. We trust Him to bring value and purpose to our storm. We remain faithful to Him. We believe He is good regardless of the circumstances we face or the outcome to those circumstances, since we know He will always be faithful to us.

GOD UNDERSTANDS

I must admit, I have reacted to life's problems in all three of the above ways. Sometimes it seems we go through one or all of the stages mentioned above. Sometimes we are so shaken and raw with emotion that we aren't able to wisely approach a storm as we ought. Sometimes we begin to grasp for solutions from sheer desperation and fear. Sometimes we feel as if God is the cause of our storm and our anger drives us far from Him. Sometimes we feel we are the cause of our own storm and God would not be willing to forgive us, let alone help us.

I think God understands that. All of that. He can look into our hearts.

The way we face storms can be like what are called the five stages of grieving: Denial, Anger, Bargaining, Depression, and Acceptance. I'm not a counselor, so I don't know how valid those are, but it seems that at times we do progress through a series of reactions to our storms.

God knows we are dust. After all, He was the One who formed us from dust. He knows how frail we can be.

God would love for us to choose the third option first and turn to Him in trust, but He'll take us right at the point from which we do decide to turn to Him and finally ask for help. So if you are currently utilizing option one or two, it's not too late to change to option three!

It pleases God when you turn to Him. He wants you to trust Him. He wants to help you.

Turning to God greatly benefits you also. It builds your faith. It makes you a stronger Christian. Learning to turn to God first and learning to trust Him is an ongoing process that will build your faith muscles. So as hard as it may seem to not get angry at God, or not to ignore God and trust in yourself to work out the problems, you need to turn to God.

You should be able to say with King David, *The LORD is my strength and my shield; my heart trusted in him, and I am helped: therefore my heart greatly rejoiceth; and with my song will I praise him.* Psalm 28:7

Calming Your Storm

I challenge you to allow your storms to conform you to the image of Christ.

- What is God's view of you? If you have not settled the question of whether or not you are saved and on your way to Heaven, now is the time to do it. Call your pastor or your Bible study leader. They would be happy to help you get that settled today.
- What is your view of God? Do you see God as an overly stern or an overly indulgent Father? God is a loving Father. He always has your best interest at heart. He corrects and chastises in love to draw you back to Himself. Do a study on God's love and mercy. Also check out verses on God's holiness and righteousness. Begin to develop a balanced, biblical view of God. Rather than trusting your feelings, hold fast to the truths and facts you learn about God in His Word.
- What role does God play in your storms? Do you place God in the role of bad guy? Or do you shove God out of the picture completely? God should have first place in your life. He should be the One you turn to during life's storms. Examine the role God has played in your past storms. Now determine to allow God to freely control your storms.
- Turn to God in your stormy times. Don't face life's trials alone. I found that my view of God greatly influenced my view of the storms in my life. It colored my ability to trust, to have courage, to have peace, joy, and comfort. Those are all very elusive things during a storm, but they are not impossible to obtain. God can give them all to you. And more than that, when you turn to God during the storms of your life, you will find that the storms will have an eternal and priceless value.
- Contemplate the fact that God may be allowing you to go through this storm to cause you to become more Christ-like. You may not see that right now, but that is the case. Daily ask God to help you to be more Christ-like. Oh, what a wonderful thing to be like Christ!

Memorize These Verses

Proverbs 18:10 *The name of the LORD is a strong tower: the righteous runneth into it, and is safe.*

Psalm 107:29 *He maketh the storm a calm, so that the waves thereof are still.*

Isaiah 4:6 *And there shall be a tabernacle for a shadow in the daytime from the heat, and for a place of refuge, and for a covert from storm and from rain.*

Isaiah 25:4 *For thou hast been a strength to the poor, a strength to the needy in his distress, a refuge from the storm, a shadow from the heat, when the blast of the terrible ones is as a storm against the wall.*

Prelude to the Storm

A Storm Is Brewing

On the morning of July 19, 1999, I thought that my greatest trial was a financial one. By evening, it was the least of my worries. But first, let me back up and explain a bit.

For almost thirty years my husband, Gary, and I traveled across the United States conducting Evangelistic meetings. We lived in a travel trailer year-round. We didn't own a house and we had no desire to own one. We rarely took a paycheck and never really missed having money. Somehow the Lord always took care of our needs and it was exciting to see how the Lord would provide.

We loved to travel and minister in churches. As far as we were concerned, we wanted to continue doing so for the rest of our lives or until we physically could not.

Then in 1994, God changed our hearts. Almost overnight He took away the desire to travel and placed within both of us the desire to stay put. All of a sudden we wanted a home. We wanted to settle down. We didn't want to travel anymore.

This was extremely confusing to us. We were baffled that God would change our ministry. We didn't understand why this had happened. Had we done something wrong? Was God finished with us?

We found it frightening to think God might not want us in the ministry anymore. We racked our brains trying to think of what we had done wrong. But we could not see ahead to the future. We could not see that there was a very good reason God wanted us to stay put. God knew the storms that were on our horizon. He knew why He wanted us off the road, but we did not.

We prayed and asked God what He wanted us to do. We knew Gary could never be a pastor. That just wasn't the personality God had given to him. But what did God want us to do? We had no idea.

Finally we decided to wait on the Lord. It is what God asks us to do so often in His Word, but it's so hard to do, isn't it?

We still had quite a few weeks of meetings scheduled in the next several years. We couldn't just stop traveling and go buy a house. We had no money and we knew the Lord wanted us to finish ministering in the churches in which we were scheduled to hold services.

So we continued, but in our hearts we knew we were done traveling. Shortly after this happened, I began to write my first book. It was a speech text book. I majored in Speech when I was at Bob Jones University, and as we traveled I often conducted speech seminars in Christian High Schools where we ministered.

Years earlier we had home schooled our daughter, Rynda, so that she would be able to travel with us. When she got to High School, I felt it was important that she learn some basic speech skills for her college years, so I wrote a course to teach her.

When I decided to write a speech text, I dug out the materials I had developed for Rynda and began to flesh them out for the speech text that became our High School level textbook. Over the next couple of years I added texts for Junior High speech, competition speaking, drama, and Elementary level speech games, along with teachers' texts to accompany each student text.

Gary and I intended to sell these materials to home schoolers. Our plan was to print the books one at a time on our ink jet printer. We thought we could sell them to home schoolers we met in our meetings. But by the summer of 1994, we had gotten our first order for our high school textbook and it was from a Christian school. They didn't want one copy, they wanted twelve copies! We realized that we could not be printing these books on our ink jet printer. We needed to have a real print shop do the job. That's when Quality Speech Materials began.

From 1994 to 1999, we continued to travel. The back of our truck began to fill up with thousands of text books. Half of our bedroom in the trailer became a small office. We had a business on wheels. Soon schools all over the United States had begun to order from us. It slowly dawned on us that God had given us something to do when we stopped traveling. As we got more and more orders, we began to have fewer and fewer meetings.

In the spring of 1995, my parents moved from Michigan to Greenville, South Carolina. My mom's health had been getting progressively worse and I was relieved that they wanted to move south where we could spend more time with them.

The winters in South Carolina are much milder than those in Michigan, so we knew South Carolina would be our new home. We still didn't have a house, but when we were not traveling we parked our trailer in Mom and Dad's driveway.

We began to travel less and less. In 1996 Gary and my dad built us an office building on my parents' property. Finally we had a place to store our text books and house our computers, with room to grow.

Mom was still able to get around on her own in the beginning. She could do her own cooking and cleaning. She would go into Greenville three times a week to take a water aerobics class at the hospital's health center. This helped her stay as active as possible. Dad had his own workshop and loved building toys and keeping up the property which included many trees and a good sized lawn on about an acre and a half of land.

The pull to remain home in South Carolina became stronger and stronger. We began to dread hooking up the trailer and heading out. It was physically harder because of a back problem that Gary had, but it was also emotionally harder because our hearts were no longer in traveling.

In 1996 Rynda met a wonderful Christian young man named Bo and they were married the next year. Our speech books were doing well. We were finally at peace. We knew South Carolina was where God wanted us to be. Life seemed perfect.

Or, I should say, perfect, except for one thing. We wanted a house of our own. It was something that, to my shame, I was consumed with getting. I plotted and planned for ways to make more money so we could afford the payments, but the way was not clear for us to do that. Boy was I frustrated. The trailer seemed smaller every day and living in my parents' driveway was not at all part of my dream. I wanted land and a home of my own.

As I look back, it seems strange to me that I was so consumed with wanting a house. I had never really wanted one before. A house had never been important to me. I am amazed at how quickly I was caught up in such a materialistic goal for my life. But we are all human, after all. Even evangelists' wives. It doesn't take much to get our eyes off God and onto the things in life that seem so desirable.

In 1997 a good friend from Florida, Suzan, a pastor's wife who wrote some special programs that we sell to churches and schools, mentioned that she would like to develop a book on how churches could write and run their own VBS program. Since I had heard so many pastors mention how costly VBS materials could be, I thought it was a great idea.

Gary and I went to Florida for two weeks. Suzan was going to tell me all her ideas on running a VBS program. I would do the writing. Together we would figure out ways to adapt her ideas to be used in other churches. For an entire week we worked on the structure of a simple VBS program.

One day Suzan casually mentioned they had the story outlines for an Army theme VBS they had called "I'm In The Lord's Army." They had developed the story outlines themselves. As she explained to me that maybe we could include those outlines to give the people an idea of what a week's worth of stories should be like, an idea flashed in my mind. In that instant I knew we were not going to write a book on how to write your own VBS program.

I slammed my notebook closed and announced to Suzan, "We are not writing a book about writing your own VBS." Suzan looked at me in total confusion. I am sure she thought I had flipped out as I told her, "Instead, we are going to write VBS programs! We'll do all the work for the churches and we'll make it affordable!"

Suzan and I spent the next week going over the outlines. Gary and I paid her for her contribution. Then we went home and I spent the next year and a half refining and fleshing out our first VBS program called, "Operation Sword and Shield."

We were excited. We had a new and different product. We were no longer just selling speech books, now we were offering materials that would expand and extend the ministry that we had loved for so long when we traveled. Now we were offering materials churches could use to win children to Jesus Christ.

Prelude to the Storm

A Foolish Decision - A Bitter Reaction

Offering great fundamental materials was truly important to me, but I must admit that wasn't my only motive. We knew there could be lots of money made on this endeavor. We had visions of a house, a really nice house, in our heads. The logical thing to do was to start slowly and see how the product was received. But logic and desires don't always mix.

We knew that, statistically, if you send out 1,000 mailers, you can expect 10 people to respond. It didn't take us long to decide that we would send out 100,000 mailers to churches and if we only got one percent response, then we would sell about one thousand VBS programs. Since we often got a four to five percent response on our speech materials. We were positive that we would get at least four thousand sales.

Translation: It would cost lots of money to produce and send such a large mailing, but we thought it would be no problem. We were sure we would get at least one thousand orders, but we hoped for more like four to five thousand orders! That would have been enough money to pay off everything we spent, build the house of our wildest dreams, and have money to spare.

To make a long story short, it didn't happen.

We did print and send 100,000 pieces of mail. We did borrow and spend lots of money. We did have two thousand five hundred VBS programs printed and we bought the same amount of notebooks. But when all was said and done, we only sold about two hundred VBS programs that year. We defied the statistics by going so far under that it wasn't funny. We hadn't sold one percent. We had only sold point zero, zero one percent.

Needless to say, no house was purchased, not all our bills were covered, no wildest dreams. Only the income from our text books kept us afloat.

When it dawned on me that we were not going to get the sales we had assumed we would get, I was angry. To be specific, I was angry with God. Very angry.

I'm ashamed to tell you that some of my rants to God went something like this: "How could You have done this to us? I know this is Your fault! If You had wanted us to sell more VBS's it would have happened. For years we faithfully served You! There were some years when we didn't take a single paycheck! We just eked by at times to serve You! But we never wanted money. We never wanted a home. We were happy on the road. You made us want to settle down. You made us want a house! And now You won't let us get a house. In fact, now we are in debt because You didn't let us sell at least one thousand programs. What's wrong with YOU?"

I said lots of other things too. I couldn't imagine what kind of game God was playing with us. Why had He done this to us? We had been perfectly content in a trailer, traveling, making next to nothing. We had loved it! Then God changed our hearts but it seemed to me that He didn't provide for our needs.

I speak for myself when I tell you about my feelings. My husband did not seem to go through the same anguish or anger that I did. He admitted he got carried away and should have tested the market more, but it wasn't as important, nor as life shattering to him as it was to me. He was happy to learn the many lessons about our business that we really did not know, lessons that have saved us additional heartaches since that time. He didn't blame God. He knew we had created our own mess.

But I took it much harder. I was so angry and bitter. How ashamed I am to write about the things that were taking place in my heart at that time. It is not something I talk about much, even now, long after it has been settled.

How quickly my eyes were blinded by material things. I wanted a pretty house and pretty things. When I didn't get them, I became angry. How dare God withhold them from me? Everyone else had a house. And I didn't have one because I had served God for the past twenty-five years. It was His fault I didn't have a house and His fault that now it would be a long time before I would get one. Yes, I was very bitter.

DECISION TIME

There was a time when I was so angry that I told Gary I just wanted to forget God. He had rejected me, so I would reject Him! It hurts my fingers and shames my heart to type that! And I can still see the look of deep concern and fear in Gary's eyes as I said that to him.

One day as I was thinking my angry, bitter thoughts about how much I wanted all that I didn't have, the thought hit me, "Do I want things more than I want God? Am I willing to leave God behind to get what I want so badly? Is this all that God means to me?"

Prelude to the Storm

Bitterly I thought, "Why should I still serve God? Look at all I did for Him, and look how He has repaid me." But the next instant I knew that God owed me nothing. Look at all He had done for me.

For my entire life God had been so good to me. He heaped me with blessings. I was raised in a loving, Christian home. I had a wonderful Christian husband and family. I had loved serving God and traveling in the ministry. I had loved living in a trailer and had no desire for a house. What a privilege it had been to nightly stand and tell others about Jesus Christ. I loved every minute of it!

It is true that we never had much when we were on the road, but we never went without. God always provided what we needed. I had never felt before that God owed me something because of all the "sacrifices" that I was making to serve Him. I had never even felt like anything I did was a sacrifice. I had never felt that I was doing something great for God, instead I always felt that He was doing something great for me! I had felt it was a privilege to serve God.

I was definitely torn. I realized I had a big decision to make and it could change my entire life. I had never thought that I could come to a point where I considered, for even one minute, whether or not I would love and serve God. I had loved God my entire life it seemed. I had loved serving Him. I sensed this was a "point of no return" for me.

I had some hard thinking to do. Could I reject my God?

Here is what I decided after some major heart searching. This is my journal entry from May 13, 1999.

What a spiritual struggle these past few months have been! I have been a Christian for almost 40 years, I am an evangelist's wife, and yet knowing God's will and trusting God are still so difficult!

For so long we have felt unsettled. We grope until we think we have found an answer, then it seems the answer has been kicked out from under us. I do not understand God. I no longer feel very confident in my ability to discern God's will. I don't know what God wants for us.

One thing I do know, no matter what, I still need God! I need to love Him. I need to believe that somehow He is still in control, that He still guides me.

Maybe I'll never know until eternity why all this has happened, but I find I want to put aside my anger with God and my bitter disappointment. I want to trust. Above all, I can't live without God.

Job 13:15 Though he slay me, yet will I trust in him.

With many tears I finally settled it with God. I couldn't stay angry and bitter at the One whom I had loved for so long. The One who had loved me longer.

Yes, I still struggled with the questions I had. And I still wanted a house. But I wanted God more. God was my life. I had been saved when I was four years old. I had been raised to love and serve God. I had married a preacher and we had served God together. My heart had always been tender toward God. It had been my great joy to serve God. I truly loved God. I didn't want to be bitter and angry anymore. I wasn't about to toss my God out the window in exchange for a house.

God owed me nothing. It had been no sacrifice to serve Him. It had been the greatest privilege of my life! And oh, how much He had done for me! I didn't deserve any of His love or blessings, but He constantly heaped them on me.

I could live without a house, but I could not live without God. It would be an empty life that wasn't worth living. I loved God, and all my bitterness could not take away that love.

But then a new feeling washed over me. I was so ashamed of myself. How could I have ever felt such terrible things? How could God forgive me when He looked at my ugly, bitter feelings? How could He forgive me for seriously contemplating throwing Him away?

I felt such grief about my thoughts and actions. I knew God would forgive me. He is so loving and merciful. But I felt a deep sorrow for the fact that I could even think such things.

Let me tell you, this was a terrible type of grief. It may sound crazy to have almost lost my faith over a mere pile of bricks and wood and drywall, but that was the case. It grieved me when I came to my senses and it grieves me even now to know how weak and foolish and sinful I can be.

I am honest enough to know that such ugly feelings and thoughts dwell inside of me. I am so sinful. But that's why Jesus died for me. Oh, how much I have to be thankful for to Him!

So finally, I had peace again. But we also had bills that did not go away. Financially we struggled. We had been completely debt free before the VBS fiasco, but not anymore. And financial bondage is a terrible trial also.

Yet even in this, looking back, I can see that though it was my greed that caused our debt, God had a purpose for even that. I totally believe that God did not allow us to sell that one percent for a couple of very

Prelude to the Storm

good reasons that I will tell you about later. We now regularly get at least a one percent response or greater. But I believe God didn't want us to get rich quick. And He had a reason.

In 1999, we only had thirteen weeks of meetings. That meant the rest of the year we were living in my parents' driveway in our trailer. We were working out of our office that we had built in the woods behind their house. And though my dad was in good health, my mom had been feeling poorly for the first half of the year.

On July 4th my mom had a heart attack. She was almost 83 years old and because of her general poor health, there was nothing much the doctors could do to help her condition. She would just have to live with a bad heart. Two weeks later, on July 18, the doctors gave her a bunch of new medications and sent her home to recover as best she could.

So, as I said when I started this chapter, July 19, 1999 started out normally. Mom was home from the hospital and I was trying to help as much as possible. I was cooking meals and keeping the house.

Around 5:30 PM Gary came into the house and asked me to come outside for a minute. My parents were in the living room. We had just finished dinner. I followed Gary outside wondering what he needed to tell me that he couldn't say to me while I was loading the dishwasher.

"Rynda just called," Gary said. "We need to go to the hospital. The doctor just told them that Bo has leukemia."

It is strange how many thoughts can go through your head in just a few seconds of time. In the space of about four or five seconds I remember thinking: "This can't be real," and "How could I ever be angry with God about something so unimportant as money?" and "This has got to be a terrible mistake!" and "I don't think we should tell Mom and Dad. It would upset them and Mom just got home from the hospital," and "I don't think I can breathe," and "Surely they will find they got the wrong results!" And probably a few other things.

I do distinctly remember the feeling of all my anger toward God, for I still struggled a bit, flowing down my body, out the bottoms of my feet, into the ground. My anger left me more completely and fully at that moment than anything I have ever experienced before in my life. From that moment on I have never again been angry at God about the "VBS fiasco." I just felt a strange sort of humble feeling that I can't explain. And I felt a pain of such magnitude that I have never before experienced.

Now, when I look at the spot where I was standing when I got the news of Bo's cancer, I still think, "That is the spot where I learned what is and what isn't important in life."

PREPARED FOR THE STORM

The storm had hit. And I was sure this one would sweep me off my feet for good. I wasn't angry this time. I was scared and heartbroken.

Yet as I look back now, I can see how God, in His great love, was preparing me for this storm. I look back at a diary entry that I made about a month before we found out about Bo's cancer. I know I was thinking about our financial problems, but these thoughts were preparing me for a whole new set of problems I had no way of knowing I would have to face.

June 24, 1999

Life is filled with problems. They are, perhaps, life's one constant. I think God is interested in how we handle those problems.

We can pretend the problems do not exist - bury our heads and hearts in the sand, hoping the problem will disappear by the time we come up for air.

We can shake our fist at the problem and at God, allowing anger and disappointment to consume us.

Or we can become problem solvers looking for solutions, or better yet, allowing God to provide solutions.

I believe God allows us to have problems to strengthen us, to help us to grow, to cause us to become more Christ-like.

Lord,

When I am faced with a problem, old or new, help me to be a problem solver. Help me to have the courage to face my problems. Help me to have the faith to know the problem is given by Your permission, not to crush me, but to strengthen and teach me.

Help me to trust that there are no problems I cannot handle as long as I have Your help and guidance.

When I long for a problem-free life, help me to remember the value of the problems I have already faced. Help me to remember that in the past You have always proved Yourself to be a trustworthy and faithful friend.

Thank you that in every problem I have ever faced or ever will face, You are by my side. I am not alone.

I see now that God was preparing me for the storm that was brewing. I didn't see the dark clouds on the horizon, they were still too distant for my eyes to see, but God knew what lay ahead. He had begun to prepare my heart.

Lessons I Learned

I learned several lessons following the "VBS Fiasco." Let me share a few of them with you.

Avoid storms when possible.
Almost everyone's natural inclination is to avoid all storms. Except, of course, those who love to study storms. Storm Chasers. They drive frantically toward storms in an effort to experience the storm up close and personal.

But that's not what most folks do. When you see a storm coming you try to avoid it. And if you can't avoid the storm, then you try to find a way out of the storm as soon as possible.

No one in their right mind wants to have troubles and trials. We all want to avoid storms, don't we? Sure. There's nothing wrong with that. But that's not what I am talking about when I talk about avoiding storms. I'm not talking about avoiding the unavoidable. Some storms are unavoidable. But at times, storms can be avoided.

I know that is a fact because, as I described before, there have been times in my life when I have caused my own storms, like the financial storm we faced when we rushed ahead of God's timing and took matters into our own hands. Sure, I blamed God for that storm, but I know that I caused my own storm. It could have easily been avoided if only I had waited for God's timing instead of rushing ahead and doing what I felt was best to achieve my own goals.

The Bible tells us to wait on the Lord. It is a sin not to wait on God's timing. And sin will cause many of our storms. But I'm not just talking about the sin of not waiting on God. There are many other sins that entangle and confound our lives. Sin always causes us to suffer. We don't often like to admit it, but when we sin, we cause our own storms.

The summer that Rynda turned six years old, we spent about eight weeks ministering in Alaska. Gary, Rynda, and I each had one suitcase apiece for clothes, plus a suitcase full of toys for Rynda, and a few pieces of equipment for our meetings. We had a full schedule of services that we would be conducting in the logging camps. Everything we took had to be very compact since all of our travel would be in a small Cessna float plane.

Once the luggage had been loaded, the three of us and our missionary pilot squeezed in and tried to get the best view out the small windows as possible. It was fascinating to look down on the whales as they frolicked in the ocean and the enormous glaciers with cracks large enough that the plane could have landed inside one of them. The views were breathtaking.

One day as we flew toward the next logging camp where we were scheduled to spend the week, we noticed a strange thing ahead of us in the sky. I pointed to a dark cloud that seemed to hover over a small area ahead of us. It looked like a sheer curtain that extended from the cloud on down to the land below.

The pilot explained that it was raining there. How strange it was to see rain from such a different vantage point. From our perspective we could see the storm ahead while all around that area there was sunshine.

The pilot assured us we did not have to worry. Because he could see the problem ahead, he would merely take a small detour around the rain and we could continue on our way. We would not have to fly through the storm. We could avoid it completely.

God knows the storms that come about because of sin. That is why He has given us the Bible. It tells us how to avoid sin. It gives a way to detour around the sins that threaten us. It tells us how to avoid the sin which causes many of our storms.

If we spend time studying the Bible, then we can become Storm Detectors instead of Storm Chasers. We can detour around the storms instead of rushing headlong toward them. The Bible will help us avoid so many unnecessary problems and heartaches by learning to obey God and waiting on His will, His way, and His time.

Be honest.

How easily we can deceive ourselves. And Satan loves to deceive us, if we let him. I learned that in my desire to obtain what I wanted in life, I often was not honest with myself or with God.

Let me share with you an amusing but true story from my childhood. I call it, "The National Anthem of Siam."

Prelude to the Storm

Every summer I loved to go to our family cottage on Wampler's Lake.

Sometimes our whole extended family would gather for a day of swimming, eating, and just plain fun. I had lots of cousins and we enjoyed the warm summer days on the lake.

One summer day as we cousins searched for something to occupy our afternoon, my older brother's wife, Angie, decided to spend some time with us.

Angie was full of ideas for fun games. She came up with several fun things to occupy our time. Then she hit on a great idea. She would teach us young cousins a song that we could sing for our parents after the cookout that night. She explained that it was a song in another language but she was sure we could learn it. It was the National Anthem of Siam.

That appealed to everyone. We would learn to sing an important song in another language. How impressive! We cousins were all certain that our parents were sure to be impressed also! We eagerly agreed.

Phrase by phrase Angie taught us the words. We practiced them slowly until we began to get the swing of it. The music was easy. It was sung to the tune of "My Country Tis Of Thee."

The words went like this. "O wa ta goo Siam."

Over and over we practiced placing the right word with the right note of the song. "O wa ta goo Siam. O wa ta goo Siam. O wa ta goo."

Finally we all felt that we could do a very respectable job of singing the song. We were able to pick up speed and sing right along to the end of the song.

The moment came for us to perform for the adults. All the cousins lined up in the front of the cabin and stood up tall. Angie stood in the back, apparently not wanting to steal any of the attention. I stepped forward to announce that as a special treat we had learned a song to sing for the adults. I proudly proclaimed it to be the National Anthem of Siam. Then I stepped back in line and with a nod from Angie, the cousins began to belt out the song.

At first the adults listened politely. But then a strange thing happened. As the song progressed, the adults began to react in the strangest manner. First there were smiles and then soft laughs.

I was puzzled by the laughter. Why on earth would they laugh? Obviously they did not appreciate all the time and effort we had put into learning this noble song. And how disrespectful to the country of Siam!

As the song progressed, the adults began to laugh louder and harder. The louder and harder the adults laughed, the louder and faster we cousins sang on. Finally we came to the last line and our parents were all but rolling on the floor.

"O wa ta goo Siam. O wa ta goo Siam. O wa ta gooose. O what a goose I am. O what a goose I am. O whaaat a goose I am. Ooo what a gooooooose!"

With a flourish the song ended, and at about the last line of the song we cousins all finally heard ourselves singing, "O what a goose I am!"

There stood Angie, laughing right along with the rest of the adults. And we all had to admit, it was funny. Here we had been so proud to be learning the National Anthem of Siam. How easily we had been deceived!

Satan is good at deceiving people. He can make them believe a total lie and they often don't even know that they have been tricked. At least not until it is too late.

We can be pretty good at deceiving ourselves too. I know. I was good at it when it came to denying my own fault in the problems I was facing. It was easier to blame God than to face reality.

After the "VBS Fiasco" it took me a long time to be honest with myself. Even after I had put my anger and bitterness behind me, I still didn't want to think about, let alone voice, the fact that I had been so foolish.

I didn't want to face the fact that I could so easily be sidetracked from God's will for my life. I had loved the Lord since I was a young child. I had been an evangelist's wife for twenty-five years. I had completely devoted my life to serving the Lord. I loved serving the Lord. I felt I should have been above all those human emotions and motives that propelled me toward a near disaster with my faith.

I was truly appalled when I realized I had so quickly turned from wanting to serve God to wanting God to serve me. But I am human. I have no supernatural spiritual powers that exempt me from being so easily led astray by all the shiny things that tempt all humans.

Before the "VBS Fiasco" Gary and I always had this motto: If we don't have the money, we don't buy it. That was a good motto and one we have returned to. I believe God honors that. It certainly goes a long way toward calming financial storms!

I think we all have certain sins and weaknesses we battle, sometimes daily. The Bible lists them: the lust of the flesh, the lust of the eyes, and the pride of life. It seems we all have something with which we are truly tempted. It is only honest to admit that. But it certainly isn't easy. Yet, facing our life honestly can be the first step in winning our own personal battles and overcoming the storms we face.

Being honest with myself was my first step in facing the financial storm we faced. But more importantly, it was the first step in facing the spiritual storm I was going through.

Sometimes we need to be honest with ourselves. No, not all storms are caused by our own sinful decisions, but some of them are. And often we have the gall to shake our fists at God and blame Him when all along we are to blame.

Not all storms are of our own making, but if the storm you face is caused by your own foolish and sinful self, then the sooner you admit it, the sooner you and God can work on the solution.

Galatians 6:7 says, *Be not deceived; God is not mocked: for whatsoever a man soweth, that shall he also reap.*

Wait on the Lord.

I hate to wait. I am the type of person who makes up my mind about what I want, then I instantly want it to happen. I have a hard time stepping back and giving things time to work out.

When I see God's direction in my life, I want things to happen now. When God led us to want to settle down, I wanted to go off the road that week. I knew we couldn't stop traveling for several years to come, but it was so hard to continue to travel when I no longer had the desire. When the Lord put a desire for a house in my heart, I couldn't wait to buy a house. I didn't want to wait. Since God had not shown me how we would ever get the money to pay for the house, I decided to find my own way. I didn't say that in so many words, but I felt it and spent my time trying to make my goals come about. Now, I wish I had waited on God. Being so impatient has caused it's share of problems. But as they say, hind sight is 20/20.

Fortunately, God has allowed me to learn from my mistakes and alter my normal modus operandi. I am learning more and more about waiting.

The main lesson I have learned is that God has a perfect time for everything. And God won't be pushed.

Look at Abraham and Sarah. God promised them they would have a child. He told Abraham he would be the father of many nations. But then, it seemed like God did not fulfill His promise. Time went on and on. No child came. How frustrated they were. How empty Sarah's arms felt.

So they decided not to wait. If God could not come up with a workable plan, they would. So they rushed ahead and took matters in their own hands. Instead of waiting patiently on God, they put their plan into action. Then they spent the next few years regretting that they had not waited on God because their family situation became miserable. They faced anger, jealousy, family tension, and many other negative consequences as a result of their impatience.

Then, in God's perfect time, He gave Sarah and Abraham the promised son. But the results of their impatience continued to plague them. What regrets! Just think of how much more peace and happiness they would have experienced if they had just waited on the Lord's time.

David, on the other hand, was wise enough, even as a young man, to wait on the Lord. God anointed David to be king of Israel. But it wasn't until several years later that he was actually able to take the throne.

There were times when David could have hurried things along. He had the opportunity to remove King Saul by his own doings, but he would not rush ahead of God. Instead, he was content to do things God's way. And for his obedience, he was rewarded by God with a prosperous kingdom and a clear conscience. He didn't have to look back and regret his actions.

It's not that I think it was any easier for David to wait than it is for you or me.

David once expressed his frustration in Psalm 69:3 when he said, *I am weary of my crying: my throat is dried: mine eyes fail while I wait for my God.*

David found waiting to be hard but he waited anyway. Listen to some of the other things David said about waiting.

Psalm 27:14 *Wait on the LORD: be of good courage, and he shall strengthen thine heart: wait, I say, on the LORD.*

Psalm 37:7, 9 *Rest in the LORD, and wait patiently for him: fret not thyself because of him who prospereth in his way, because of the man who bringeth wicked devices to pass. For evildoers shall be cut off: but those that wait upon the LORD, they shall inherit the earth.*

Psalm 37:34 *Wait on the LORD, and keep his way, and he shall exalt thee to inherit the land: when the wicked are cut off, thou shalt see it.*

Psalm 59:9 *Because of his strength will I wait upon thee: for God is my defence.*

I think God wants us to wait for a reason. Here are a couple of reasons that I see.

First, God's time is best. It's that simple. God knows what should be done and the perfect time to do it. He is the One who knows what is best. He is the One who is in control. He can see ahead. We can't.

When we don't wait on Him, we are trying to jerk control out of His hands. Yet all we really succeed in doing is making a mess. We would be wise to learn that if we wait on God's time, then things will work out exactly as God plans.

Psalm 69:6 says, *Let not them that wait on thee, O Lord GOD of hosts, be ashamed for my sake: let not those that seek thee be confounded for my sake, O God of Israel.*

Secondly, God wants us to wait on Him so we can learn to submit to Him. When we wait on God, we are showing our submission to Him. We are saying, "I will not rush ahead and do things my way. Instead I will wait and do things Your way. You know what is best. I give You control."

Psalm 62:5 says, *My soul, wait thou only upon God; for my expectation is from him.*

In the society in which we live, not many people are very anxious to submit to anyone. We don't want others telling us what to do. Wives don't like to submit to their husbands. Children don't like to submit to their parents. Employees don't like submitting to their bosses. As a result, we have a hard time submitting to God. We don't want to hand the control of our lives to anyone, not even God.

Sometimes it is hard to submit because we are stubborn and want things our own way. But stubbornness may not be the only reason we don't want to submit to God.

Submitting to God can be extremely hard when we are filled with fear. Storms cause fear. And fear often causes us to try to take matters into our own hands rather than waiting on God. We struggle to find answers and solutions. We reach out in fear for the first thing that seems to offer relief.

The answer to fear is trust. It takes trust to submit to someone else. What if they are wrong? What if they are untrustworthy?

In the next chapter we will talk about trust in the storm. We will go into more depth about why God is worthy of our trust. We'll discuss why we can submit complete control to Him and know that He is worthy of our trust and He is always right.

But regardless of our reasons for not waiting on God, not waiting is always the wrong choice. Let me assure you, it is worth it to wait on God. Take it from someone who has some very serious regrets about not waiting on God. Learn to wait and you'll never regret it.

Isaiah 40:31 says, *But they that wait upon the LORD shall renew their strength; they shall mount up with wings as eagles; they shall run, and not be weary; and they shall walk, and not faint.*

Lamentations 3:25-26 says, *The LORD is good unto them that wait for him, to the soul that seeketh him. It is good that a man should both hope and quietly wait for the salvation of the LORD.*

Plan for the storm.

Some storms show up on the horizon and you can see the dark clouds gathering and moving your way. Other storms seemingly rise out of nowhere and blind-side you. While you can never tell when a storm will come, one thing I can tell you with a reasonable degree of certainty, you will face a storm someday.

Count on it. In fact, plan for it!

And by "plan," I mean "prepare." You can't often choose your storms. And God doesn't want us to spend our time wringing our hands and worrying about an unseen storm. I'm not suggesting a pre-storm panic fest. Don't be like the person who said, "Worrying must work! Almost everything I worry about never happens!" But you can prepare for storms in a manner that would be pleasing to God.

In 1991 Gary and I were happily traveling from city to city. We would conduct a week of evangelistic services in one church, then we would pack up and head to the next church to begin all over again the next week. Back then our lives were total freedom to us. We were as happy as two clams.

One week in June of 1991 we were at a church in Ohio. We had just backed the trailer into a spot beside the Pastor's house and were preparing to unhook the trailer. Gary lifted his leg to step from one side of the hitch to the other when his foot got tangled in the wires that ran between the truck and trailer. I grabbed for him, but it was too late. Gary fell on his face but his tangled foot remained up in the wires over the hitch.

Prelude to the Storm

He wrenched his back badly and he was in a lot of pain. We began to make the rounds to different doctors and chiropractors. Being on the road meant a different doctor every week. The summer dragged on and by August we still had no answers about how to help him. His back seemed okay, but he had a pain that radiated down his leg. Most of the time he just kept going, took aspirin, and tried to ignore the pain. Sometimes his pain was so bad that he had to sit on a stool to preach.

Two weeks before Thanksgiving, Gary was outside the trailer doing some woodworking. In the late afternoon he decided to come into the trailer to get ready for the evening service. He opened the door, but found he couldn't lift his leg as far as the first step. So he crawled in.

As he crawled into the trailer on his hands and knees, I took one look at his face, which was as white as a sheet, and I began to look for blood. I was certain he had cut his hand off with the saw. But there was no blood. He just couldn't move.

As he lay in the middle of the floor, he told me he would be fine in a few minutes and that I shouldn't call the pastor because he would definitely be able to preach that night. I had my doubts. When I found he couldn't even roll over, I stepped over him and went to call the Pastor to explain our problem. Even though Gary continued to protest that he would be fine in a few minutes, he was in no position to stop me. Services for that evening were cancelled.

The next morning the pastor helped me load Gary into his car and it only took the doctor one look for him to tell us that Gary had a ruptured disc. Now we knew. Gary needed back surgery and the doctor said there was a possibility he might also have permanent nerve damage since it had taken so long to diagnose it.

When Gary and I got back to the trailer, we knew we had a big storm ahead of us. There were some major areas we could see that could cause trouble in the days ahead.

First, the rest of our meetings for several months to come had to be canceled. It would be months before we would have an income again.

Also, it was winter and we couldn't live in the trailer in the bitter cold of Michigan, so we would have to move in with my parents. We would live in my old bedroom before and after Gary's surgery. It would mean extremely close quarters for all of us for about six months.

It was November when Gary was diagnosed, but a trip to the Neurosurgeon let us know that it wouldn't be until February before the surgery would occur. Then there would be several months of recovery and rehab. This was not a fast process.

A long, unknown trial lay ahead of us and we were frightened. How would we pay our bills? What if Gary had permanent damage and ended up in a wheelchair? Would we ever be able to travel again?

We looked at each other, Gary laying on the floor and me sitting on the couch, and we did something I am so thankful the Lord gave us the wisdom to do that day. As we talked about all the unknowns that lay ahead, we decided to make a pact with each other and with God.

We said, "Lord, we don't know how any of this is going to come out, but we do know that You are in control. We are making a pact right now, with You and with each other, that no matter what happens, we will trust You. Please don't let anything tear apart our love for You or our love for each other. The three of us are in this together."

That was the simple pact we made. And God honored it.

It was a very long six months. The quarters were tight. The waiting seemed endless. But we came through it with our trust in God and our relationship not only in tact, but actually stronger.

Our storm had already begun when we made decisions about how we would face our storm, and it is something we have since said that we will do when any new storm comes along.

Whether you are alone in life or are fortunate enough to have someone to face the storm with you, you would be wise to make such a pact with God when a storm hits. Determine ahead of time to face the storm in such a way that God would be honored and your faith would grow and strengthen.

GOD IS THE JUDGE

Let me also add a quick word to those of you who are snug and warm inside, settled by the fire and far from the storm that rages outside. When you look out your window and see a fellow Christian as he leans into the blasting wind and struggles to weather a storm, do not assume that it is his own sin that has caused the storm. Instead, offer him some warmth and a helping hand.

Why? Because not all storms are caused by sin. Remember in the Bible when a man was blind and the disciples asked Jesus, "Who sinned that this man is blind? Him or his parents?"

Jesus answered, "Neither. He was born blind so that I would get the glory."

I once knew some people who were quick to pin the blame for every storm in others' lives on sin. Whenever something went wrong they would very righteously, but somewhat gleefully, say, "See, they sinned. God is judging them!"

It was not their place to judge. God alone is the judge. We need to be careful about pointing fingers. But when it comes to our own life, it doesn't hurt to take a careful look and ask, "God, are you trying to tell me something?"

Not all storms are our fault. Not all storms are chastisement from God. Some storms come so that others can see God working in our lives and it builds their faith. Storms can come so we can see God working in our lives and it builds our own faith.

Storms come to strengthen our faith. They also come to show what a great God we love and serve. Some storms come and we may never know what purpose they serve while we are on this earth, but God knows, and sometimes faith demands that alone be enough for us.

There is so much to be learned in a storm. God allows everything for our good and for His glory. If we can only get a grasp on that fact, then the approaching storms of life will look entirely different to us. We will face them with an entirely different attitude.

CALMING YOUR STORM

I challenge you to take a close look at your life and the storms in your life. Be honest with yourself and with God.

- Are your storms avoidable? Think about it. Are there things you say and do that bring on some of your storms? Are there ways you can think of that would help you to avoid the avoidable storms so that you can have more peace in your life? First ask God to point out ways that you may not be avoiding storms. Then ask God to show you ways to detour around those storms.

- Do your storms come from sin in your life? Do some honest soul-searching. Let God point out the sin in your life. Confess that sin and ask God to help you to avoid it. It isn't easy or fun to admit that sin is in your life. But God often allows storms that trouble you for the express purpose of pointing out that sin and helping you to confess and forsake it.

- Are you waiting on God's perfect timing for your life? Many storms come about when you rush ahead of God and take matters into your own hands. Ask God for the patience to wait on Him. Spend some time in His Word reading verses about waiting on God. Notice the promises God gives to those who wait on Him.
- Do you have a plan for facing storms that includes God? Whether you can see a storm brewing or are already in the midst of a storm, you can make a pact with God to give your storms to Him to control. Talk to God about your storms. Ask Him what you should do and not do. Wait on Him to show you the answer.
- Get into God's Word. Spend some time every day getting to know your God. Find out how God wants you to handle your storms so that you will be more Christ-like.

Memorize These Verses

Psalm 139:23-24 *Search me, O God, and know my heart: try me, and know my thoughts:*

And see if there be any wicked way in me, and lead me in the way everlasting.

Lamentations 3:25-26 *The LORD is good unto them that wait for him, to the soul that seeketh him.*

It is good that a man should both hope and quietly wait for the salvation of the LORD.

Trust in the Storm

THE ISSUE OF TRUST

Of all the things I want to talk about in this book, I believe that trust in God is one of the most important things you must develop. If you can get a firm handle on trust, then you can weather any storm, no matter how fierce that storm may be.

During the time that my son-in-law was fighting leukemia, I found that there were days when I did not have much comfort or courage. There were months when I couldn't seem to find any joy in life, but as long as I had trust, I was able to hold on to the fact that there was a reason and a purpose in all that was happening. Even though I might be frightened, sad, and without much comfort, my trust in God helped me to go on.

It is important that you find who you should trust, then find a way to hang onto your trust. You probably already know that you can't trust others and you can't even trust yourself. You probably know that I am going to tell you to trust God, but you may also be wondering IF you can trust God. You need to settle that in your heart.

The rewards of trust in God are great. With trust, rather than being destroyed in the storm, you can find shelter in the storm. You can find the calm in the eye of the storm. You will be able to hang on to the fact that you have someone who completely understands what you are facing and someone who loves and cares for you as no one else can.

Trust in God brings peace. It brings hope. It is the light at the end of the tunnel. It is the thing that enables you as a Christian to say, "I have no idea why this is happening, or how I'm going to get through this, or when it will all end, but I do know that through it all I have a God who loves me, He understands, and He knows what I don't. That is enough!"

That's trust. And if you plan to make it through life's storms, you need to trust God.

So let's examine this issue of trust. Let's look at the One who is trustworthy. Let's look at how to have trust in God.

Psalm 57:1 says, *Be merciful unto me, O God, be merciful unto me: for my soul trusteth in thee: yea, in the shadow of thy wings will I make my refuge, until these calamities be overpast.*

YOU CAN'T TRUST EVERYONE

When Gary and I traveled and conducted evangelistic meetings, we were a bit different from your ordinary, everyday, run of the mill evangelistic team. In the early years we conducted meetings for children. We saw that children learned and retained information so much more readily when it was visual. Because of that, we tried to make all of our presentations as visual as possible. We called our ministry Visual Evangelism.

One way we made things visual was to use object lessons and Gospel magic tricks. While the children watched and tried to figure out, "How did they do that?" we added in the Gospel. The visuals really got across the point and aided memory.

When we began to conduct family evangelistic meetings for young and old, we never dropped the visuals. In addition to Gary's preaching at the end of the evening, we used doves and rabbits. Gary put me in chained boxes, cut me in three pieces, and chopped my head off. Gary played the Swiss Cow Bells and Rynda also played the bells and the harp. We used all sorts of visuals to teach. After all, adults love to be fooled, they love a good story, and they are really just big kids.

One of the object lessons we used involved a big, nasty rat trap. Gary would set the trap, stick his finger into it, and watch as everyone jumped in shock when it almost snapped shut on his finger. His finger escaped by a hair.

Then Gary would reset the trap and ask for a young lady to help him. He would always select a teen girl first. He would say, "I am going to tell you something that is the truth. I want to see if you believe me or not."

He would have the girl extend her pointer finger and say, "If you take that finger, bring it over and press down where the bait goes, you will not hurt your finger. That's the truth. Do you believe that?"

In the almost 30 years that Gary did that trick, only one or two teen girls said they believed him. The answer was normally, "No!" He would thank the girl and let her return to her seat.

Then Gary would ask if there was a young lady who did believe him. This time he would select a young lady that raised her hand who appeared to be about ten or eleven years old. When she got to the platform, again he would have the girl extend her finger and he would say, "Do you believe me when I say you won't hurt your finger if you put it in the rat trap?" Most girls would say, "Yes, I believe you." Then he would say, "I'm going to tell you the same thing I told the last girl. If you bring that finger over and put it where the bait goes and press down, you will not hurt your finger. You said you believed me. Are you willing to put your finger in the trap?"

Nine times out of ten the girl would pull her finger back and say, "No."

"Do you know what that tells me?" Gary would ask. "It tells me she doesn't really believe me."

Gary would thank the girl, have her sit down and then ask for a girl who not only believed him, but was willing to put her finger in the trap.

By this time the number of volunteers would have been greatly reduced. But usually there was a wee hand or two that would still go up. This time Gary would pick a girl about four or five years old.

Up she would come and again with the finger extended Gary would say, "If you really believe me, I want you to put your finger where the bait goes, press down, and leave it there. Don't try to beat it out."

And it was with amazement and a bit of fear that the entire crowd of onlookers would watch as that precious little one would, without hesitation, stick her finger into the trap and press down where the bait went.

And all would be fine. She didn't get hurt.

"Do you know what that tells me?" Gary would ask. "It tells me she not only believes me, she also trusts me. There is a big difference between belief and trust. Not a single one of these young ladies would have been hurt. The first young lady wasn't willing to believe me. The second said she believed me but she didn't trust me. But this young lady truly believes me. It took trust for her to stick her finger in the trap."

It almost always worked that way. Gary would point out that the older we get the less trusting we are. We learn that you can't always trust what people say. And the harder it is to trust people, the harder it is to trust God.

How true.

You can't trust everyone and it would be foolish and naive to think that you can. When you are young, you are very trusting. Then someone lies to you or steals from you or breaks a promise. You learn that you cannot always trust people.

Unfortunately, when we lose trust in people we often lose trust in God. But God is not a mere human. He is perfect and He cannot go against His Holy Word or His righteous self.

WHO CAN YOU TRUST?

Some people only want to trust themselves. They think that with their own wits, or strength, or money they can overcome all obstacles. They think that even if they can't trust others, at least they can trust themselves.

It is easy for Christians to fall into the same faulty thinking. We like to solve our own problems. We like to figure out the way we want things to work out and then try to find a way to make it happen.

I am somewhat of a control freak. When I see an obstacle in life my first thought is usually, "Hmm. How can I make this come out the way I think is best?" And I usually have an answer close at hand. If I can't implement the solution by myself, then I go to God and say, "Lord, I have this problem. Please help me. Here's what You need to do. . ."

God must listen and frown. Or perhaps He smiles indulgently. Then He, in His wisdom and kindness says, "I have a better way. A much better way!"

And God's way is always better. Much better!

I have learned that it is foolish to think my way is best. That's why I often tell God, "Don't listen to me. When I come up with some crazy scheme, just ignore me and do what You know is best!"

I have seen God work things out in such a different manner than I would have chosen and He brings about such a different ending than I would have ever dreamed of, and yet when it was all done I saw that His way truly was so much better than mine would have been.

Can I honestly make that statement, even when an ending involves something like the death of my dear son-in-law? Yes. Even in that ending, which I would never have chosen in a million years, God's way has proven to be best.

I won't tell you that I have trusted in every storm I have faced. You know, if you read chapter two, that the financial storm in my life made me so angry and bitter with God that I was totally ready to jerk all control out of God's hands and take matters into my own. Not only did I not trust God, I was ready to reject God completely. But when I did finally come to a place of trust, what a relief it was to let God have control and not feel I had to come up with all the right answers. And my trust was not misplaced. God was faithful, even after the way I had reacted initially to my storm.

Neither you nor anyone else is worthy of trust.

Psalm 118:8-9 says, *It is better to trust in the LORD than to put confidence in man. It is better to trust in the LORD than to put confidence in princes.*

Psalm 146:3 says, *Put not your trust in princes, nor in the son of man, in whom there is no help.*

We humans are all fallible. We make mistakes. We break promises. We don't understand many things. We don't have much power to control life's circumstances.

But God does.

God Is Trustworthy

Okay. You know, in your head, that God is trustworthy. You believe and trust He has forgiven your sin and will take you to Heaven. But to trust God completely with your life here on earth can be another matter entirely.

We know in our mind we can trust God. But because we are still human we often don't truly understand how anyone, even God, can be completely trusted. That is where faith comes in. God asks us to have the faith to trust our lives to His care.

We know we should trust God, but it sure is hard to sit back and have faith that He will do the best thing at the best time.

I understand that. I know that, if it were possible, I would absolutely love to be in complete control of my life. Call me up any time and I can tell you exactly how I think the next few months and years should go in my life. I love making lists and writing down appointments. I love to plan where the path ahead should go and what should happen along the way. And never once have I planned for a bump in the road, let alone a major storm. I like things tied up in a neat little package with a pretty little bow.

It is very hard for me to take my hands off of my life and sit back and say, "Okay, God. I'll give You control. I'll trust You to do what is best for my good and Your glory."

I'm more likely to say, "But God, I'm afraid to give You control. What if Your will is something I don't like? What if Your will changes my life completely? It's scary to trust You!"

But trust demands that we have faith. It demands that we put aside what we feel about the storm we face and instead look at what we know to be true about our God. Trust is less about how you feel about God than it is about what you know to be true about God.

That is why it is so important to spend time in God's Word. It is where we learn the truth about God. It is our lifeline to the One who has all the answers. It builds our faith and convinces us that God can be trusted. It is our way of being certain that we have chosen the most trustworthy One.

The closer we are to God, the easier it is to accept the fact that God is trust-worthy. When we spend time getting to know God and letting Him speak to us through His Word, then we become more and more grounded in the truth of the fact that God is trustworthy. The Bible tells us He is, and the more time we spend in the Word, the more we will be convinced of that fact.

Don't look at the storm, look at God. And when you feel like you can't see God, look at God's Word. Look at what you know to be true about God. Don't expect trust to be a warm-fuzzy feeling. Instead let your trust be grounded in the knowledge of God's Word. Don't trust a feeling, trust what the Bible tells you is truth. When you are surrounded by a fog of uncertainty in life, hang on to what you know to be true about God. Trust in Him and in His Word.

When darkness veils His lovely face,
I rest on His unchanging grace.

Edward Mote

God is everywhere. He knows all. He has all power. He is in control. He is the One you should turn to in time of need. He is the only one who can truly help you.

Don't take my word for it. Read what God says about trusting Him in the Bible. Here are just a few verses. You can find more.

2 Samuel 22:31 says, *As for God, his way is perfect; the word of the LORD is tried: he is a buckler to all them that trust in him.*

Psalm 9:10 says, *And they that know thy name will put their trust in thee: for thou, LORD, hast not forsaken them that seek thee.*

Psalm 18:2 says, *The LORD is my rock, and my fortress, and my deliverer; my God, my strength, in whom I will trust; my buckler, and the horn of my salvation, and my high tower.*

Psalm 31:19 says, *Oh how great is thy goodness, which thou hast laid up for them that fear thee; which thou hast wrought for them that trust in thee before the sons of men!*

Psalm 34:22 says, *The LORD redeemeth the soul of his servants: and none of them that trust in him shall be desolate.*

Psalm 36:7 says, *How excellent is thy lovingkindness, O God! therefore the children of men put their trust under the shadow of thy wings.*

Psalm 37:3 says, *Trust in the LORD, and do good; so shalt thou dwell in the land, and verily thou shalt be fed.*

Psalm 37:5 says, *Commit thy way unto the LORD; trust also in him; and he shall bring it to pass.*

Psalm 125:1 says, *They that trust in the LORD shall be as mount Zion, which cannot be removed, but abideth for ever.*

Those are just a few verses about what you can be assured of if you put your trust in God. There are many, many more verses where God tells us why we can trust Him.

Think about what God is saying in those verses. Read them again. He is saying that when you put your trust in Him, His goodness and lovingkindness is yours. You can trust Him because His way is perfect, because He is a rock, a fortress, a deliverer. He says that those who trust Him will never be desolate, they'll never be forsaken, they'll be cared for, they'll be unmovable.

You can trust God. You have His Word on it!

God Chooses Our Storms

Some people get downright angry with God when they realize He allows or at times brings hardship into their life. They say, "If God is so loving, why on earth would He allow this?"

I admit, there have been times I have gotten angry with God. But thankfully, I haven't stayed angry. Instead, I try to work on trusting that God has a purpose for each storm, even if I can't see His purpose.

There are times when God allows us to see why a storm has occurred. Afterwards we can look back and say, "Oh! Now I see why that happened. It's a good thing it did happen. God's way was best after all!"

But there are also storms we can look at up and down, inside and out, forwards and backwards, and still not figure out why God allowed them to happen or what earthly good they did for us or for anyone.

There are things we will never know. Not in this life at least. But when we get to Heaven, then we will know. In the meantime, we just need to trust that even though we do not know, God knows. Faith says, "That's good enough for me."

That may not seem like a good answer, but it is the truth. God isn't required to let us know all the answers. He is God and He doesn't owe us an explanation. He has His reasons and I have learned that I don't have to understand everything. I would rather say, "I can trust God to do what is best for my good and His glory even if I never understand it here on earth."

So it boils down to this, there are two approaches you can take to the idea that God chooses the storms that come into your life.

1. You can be angry God would do such a thing. You can feel that if God loves you He would eliminate all storms.

2. You can trust God to do what is best for your good and His glory.

That's it in a nutshell. Which way will you choose?

I Am Not God

Here's a saying that I have no idea who said it, but it is very true. "God is God, and I am not."

That's a saying I repeat when I am having a hard time trusting. I am not God. But my God is God and I can just relax and let Him be God. I don't have to worry that He'll mess things up. I would worry about that if I were in control of my own storms. But with God in control, it is out of my hands and that is a relief.

Isaiah 26:4 says, *Trust ye in the LORD for ever: for in the LORD JEHOVAH is everlasting strength.*

When I was young I couldn't understand what on earth my parents liked about watching the news on TV. It was usually always bad news and, worst of all, it was just plain old boring. How could they sit and watch it night after night? But every night they did.

However, there was one part of the news I did like to watch. If I were in the room when it came on, up would come my head and my attention was riveted.

I liked to watch the weather report. Now, it wasn't because I cared in the least what the current temperature was, or if the barometer was rising, or even what the weather would be like the next day.

Back in the 1960's the weather reports were rarely accurate. In fact, for the most part, those reports were almost always wrong. The weathermen didn't have live, Super, Duper Doppler. They didn't have all the sophisticated radar storm tracking equipment they have today.

They could not accurately predict the weather temperatures for the next seven days. They couldn't accurately predict the weather for the next three days. In fact, they often got the weather for that day wrong!

I suspect that most days they just stuck their head out of the studio door to see what was actually happening, then ran in to report it on the air. Then they would make an educated guess about what might happen for the next day's weather.

But the fact that the weather reporters were rarely correct did not stop people from believing that maybe, some day, they might get it right. My mother believed what the reporter told her. If the weatherman said the next day would be cold and rainy with the possibility of mixed snow, then the next morning I was sent off to school bundled up in my warmest sweater, coat, mittens, hat, and boots, regardless of the fact that the sun was shining brightly and the temperature was already climbing into the 60's. If the weatherman said it, then it must be true!

No, the weather itself was not the reason I found the weather report so fascinating. What captured my attention was the weatherman, Sonny Eliot.

The Eye of the Storm

Sonny Eliot was Detroit's own local weatherman and he was a very unique individual. Sonny made the news fun to watch. He wasn't often correct about his predictions, but he was always amusing.

Sonny didn't give the weather report any more accurately than any other weatherman of the day, but he did so much more than just stand and predict the weather.

Sonny would stand in front of a flat, paper map that hung on the wall. It was not on a television monitor and there were no moving graphics of clouds or rain. There was no radar to track storms. No live view cameras showed current conditions outside. Just that flat paper map.

If the sun was shining, Sonny would slap a cut out cardboard sun with a smiley face on the map. If rain was the expected outcome, then Sonny would slap a little cardboard umbrella on the area of the map where they expected rain.

You never knew what new word Sonny would make up to describe the coming weather. If the morning was supposed to be rainy and foggy, he would proclaim that "Froggy" weather was on its way. If a mixture of snow and drizzle was expected, Sonny would warn us that we could expect "Snizzle."

Sonny always had a joke to tell. Sometimes it was just plain corny, but it was funny. Even a little girl could appreciate it.

Sonny didn't get the weather right too often, but come to think of it, even today the meteorologists, with all their fancy electronic tracking equipment and radar systems, can often be very wrong! Even though all that modern technology is available at their fingertips, the weathermen are still guessing much of the time about what will happen.

Why? Because they are not God. Only God knows for sure what the weather will be like an hour from now, a day from now, a year from now. No matter how sophisticated the equipment may become, only God knows the future.

And only God can control the future. People can guess what might happen to the world in the coming years. Some people may work hard to influence the future. But no one can control the future. No one but God.

We are only humans and we do not know why God allows things to happen. But God has a purpose for all that He does and for all that He allows to happen. God has a master plan and day by day God is working out His plan.

God has a plan for your life. He is in control of your life. Sometimes we fight God. Sometimes we disobey God. But He knows what we will think and say and do before it is ever done.

We have a choice. We can trust God to work out His plan in our lives. Or we can go kicking and screaming, fighting God every step of the way. We can choose to follow our own plan or we can tell God that we trust Him to do what is best in our lives.

Christ-Like Trust

Since I believe one of the main reasons God allows and even at times brings storms into our lives is to cause us to be more Christ-like, then I must always come back to how Christ approached the storms in His life.

Christ faced many storms while He was on earth. He was rejected by people. He was ridiculed. He experienced grief over death, over the lack of faith around Him, and over the sins He saw in others. He had physical pain. He experienced betrayal. And I could go on.

So how did Christ face His storms? Let's take a look and see what we can learn about trust from our perfect example, Jesus Christ.

Christ-like trust accepts God's Word.

Christ faced and overcame temptations by depending on God's Word. At the very beginning of His ministry, there was a time when the Bible says that Jesus was driven by the Spirit into the wilderness. He was about to go through a severe spiritual storm of testing from Satan. This was a storm that was allowed by God.

When Satan tempted Jesus with suggestions that must indeed have been true temptations to Him, Jesus drew on the Scriptures every single time to defeat Satan. He trusted God's Word to be the answer.

Matthew 4:3-4 says, *And when the tempter came to him, he said, If thou be the Son of God, command that these stones be made bread. But he answered and said, It is written, Man shall not live by bread alone, but by every word that proceedeth out of the mouth of God.*

When we face the storms of life, we must also trust that God's Word has the answers to our trials and temptations. If we want to follow the example of Christ, then we will turn to God's Word for our strength to face our storms and defeat the tempter.

2 Samuel 22:31 tells us, *As for God, his way is perfect; the word of the LORD is tried: he is a buckler to all them that trust in him.*

Christ-like trust accepts God's Will.
Christ fulfilled God's will by submission and obedience. Whenever Christ had a decision to make, He always said that He was here on earth to do His Father's will. He always referred back to what God wanted Him to do.

We don't often like to submit, but Christ willingly submitted to God's will. He constantly told others that He had not come to do His own will, but the will of God.

John 6:38 *For I came down from heaven, not to do mine own will, but the will of him that sent me.*

John 6:40 *And this is the will of him that sent me, that every one which seeth the Son, and believeth on him, may have everlasting life: and I will raise him up at the last day.*

John 9:4 *I must work the works of him that sent me, while it is day: the night cometh, when no man can work.*

During the greatest storm in Christ's life, as He faced the cross of Calvary, He once again submitted to God's will when He knelt in the garden and asked if there wasn't some other way to save mankind. But there was no other way for our sins to be forgiven. Only the blood of the perfect Lamb would do. So Christ submitted to God's will. He willingly obeyed God.

Matthew 26:38-39 says, *Then saith he unto them, My soul is exceeding sorrowful, even unto death: tarry ye here, and watch with me. And he went a little further, and fell on his face, and prayed, saying, O my Father, if it be possible, let this cup pass from me: nevertheless not as I will, but as thou wilt.*

Christ trusted His Father. He didn't have the problem that we have of not being able to see ahead to what He would face. Instead, he had the bigger problem of knowing exactly what He had to face. He knew that He would have to die on the cross and bear our sins before He ever left the glory of Heaven. Yet He showed such trust in His Father's plan.

Can you imagine what it would be like to know what lay ahead in your life? As much as we think we would like to know our future, it is a good thing we don't. We probably wouldn't get out of bed in the morning!

But it doesn't have to be as fatalistic as it sounds. Because even though we can count on storms in life, and we can't know when they will hit, or what they will bring, there is one thing we can know. We can know that every storm is allowed to cause us to become more Christ-like. That gives purpose to our storms. That gives us a reason to trust.

We also know that we do not face our storms alone. We know the One who allows the storms in our lives is by our side. Nothing can happen that God does not allow or control. His Word and His will are always for our good and His glory.

To become more Christ-like, we must face the storms in our lives with these words on our lips, "Lord, I believe Your Word is true. I accept what it says completely. And more than that, I will submit to Your will and I will obey Your voice."

Proverbs 3:5-6 says, *Trust in the Lord with all thine heart; and lean not unto thine own understanding. In all thy ways acknowledge him, and he shall direct thy paths.*

TRUST HIS HEART

There is a saying that I have always loved. I didn't know who said it for many years, but I recently found out that it is a quote from Charles Spurgeon. When I found it was attributed to him, I also found that there was an additional line added that made it even more precious. Most likely you have heard at least part of it before. It goes like this:

"God is too good to be unkind, too wise to be mistaken, and when you cannot trace His hand, you can always trust His heart."

Those are facts about God that we can, in faith, hang onto during a storm. We can always trust the heart of God to be filled with love and mercy towards us. Isn't that amazing and wonderful?

TRUST THAT GOD IS WORKING

One important lesson I have learned about trusting is that it is tremendously freeing not to have to know all of the answers. It is freeing not to have to be in control. It is freeing to be able to have the faith to believe God is at work and then just let Him work.

A Bible commentator by the name of Clarke said in one note, "How strange it is that we will neither believe that God has worked, or will work, unless we see Him working."

Trust means believing God is at work even when we are unaware of what He is doing. Trust means we have faith that God is working even when we see no evidence of His work. Trust means we can put anything in God's hands and rest in the knowledge that God is always, 100 percent of the time, working for our good and for His glory.

I'm Not Done Yet

At times you can actually watch God work things out in your life. Sometimes trust demands that you take the time to sit back and wait on Him.

At one time in my life I had a really big problem. I didn't know how to solve the problem and I didn't know what I was going to do. I felt so frustrated and discouraged.

That week I had volunteered to refinish the dining room chairs for my friend, Suzan, who is a pastor's wife in Florida. When I have problems, I find that it helps to keep my hands busy, so I got Suzan's six chairs and took them into her back yard.

I got out the bottle of chemicals that I use to strip furniture and a scrub brush and several clean cloths. I laid a plastic tarp on the ground where I was going to work. One by one I worked on the chairs, stripping away the old paint. It was hard work and I had to scrub vigorously in spite of the chemicals I was using.

It took all afternoon to remove the old finish from all six chairs. As I slowly applied the paint remover and rubbed each chair, my mind just wouldn't quit going over and over my problem. I turned it this way and that, trying to come up with a solution.

I couldn't see how I was going to solve the problem and I couldn't see how anything I could do would help. I couldn't get the worry to leave me. It just kept rubbing away at my heart and mind as I rubbed away on the chairs.

I tried praying. I begged God to help me. Did God hear me? I was sure He did, but it didn't feel like He was listening. And I didn't see how even God could solve this problem. It seemed bigger than God.

As it began to get dark I could see that, although the chairs were finally stripped clean, I would not have time to begin applying the new finish before the sun set, so I decided to finish for the evening and work some more the following day. I would apply the finish in the morning and let the chairs sit out all afternoon.

The back door was open so I went into the house. Suzan was gone. I took the chairs into the dining room and set them around the table. As I turned to walk out of the room, I glanced back and noticed how terrible the chairs looked in their half-finished condition. All the paint and varnish was stripped off and they looked dull and ugly. What would my friend think when she got home and saw all those ugly chairs in her dining room?

Without a thought, I grabbed a sheet of paper and jotted a note to attach to the chairs. As I laid the note on the table, I read the words I had written.

The note simply said. "DON'T WORRY. IT LOOKS BAD NOW, BUT I'M NOT DONE YET!"

The words of the note were a jolt to me. All day I had been praying for God to help me, to give me some answer to my prayers, but I hadn't felt like God had even heard me. Then, as I read the words, "DON'T WORRY. IT LOOKS BAD NOW, BUT I'M NOT DONE YET!" I realized that was exactly what God was saying to me.

God was speaking to my heart. He was saying, "Wendy, you have a problem, and it's too big for you, but it's not too big for me. I will work things out in My own time and in My own way. Just trust Me. I'm not done yet!"

What relief flooded my heart. Here I had spent hours and hours stewing and fretting and worrying about what would happen with my problem, but I hadn't given God a chance to work things out. God works in His own time. God works in His own way. I just needed to trust Him.

Later I found out that God had indeed been working out a solution to the problem I thought was too tough, even for Him. And He had worked it out on that very day.

Often, the problems in your life look huge. You can't solve them and you can't imagine how even God can solve them. But nothing is too big or too hard for God. You just need to remember, God works in His own time and in His own way. You just need to trust God. You need to approach your troubles in a Christ-like manner. Then have the faith to sit back and watch God work in your life.

CHOOSE TO TRUST

Trusting God is a choice. Choose to trust. And do it daily. Do it moment by moment, if necessary.

Trusting God can be hard on a normal, ho-hum day. On a stormy day it can seem totally impossible. When we see that God is not taking away all our storms or even making them as easy to navigate as we would like, then it takes real trust to say, "God, I know You are in control and You know what is best. I trust that You have a purpose for this storm."

It's hard to say that to God, but believe me, it is the best way.

It is best to choose to trust God. It is best to work at trusting God. And I do mean work, because it may take some hard work on your part to choose trust. It was hard for me. It's still hard for me. I still struggle with trust at times. I have to remind myself of the truth of what I know about God. I have to take the time to remember how God has been trustworthy in the past. I have to force my finger off of the panic button and instead bow my knees and my heart in prayer telling God that I am willing for Him to have His will.

Many of the verses on trust say, "I will. . ." That's a choice. The verses don't say, "I have to trust because God is forcing me." Trust is a day by day decision that God will not force on you. It is your choice to make.

Job made that choice even when he could make no sense out of the terrible things that had happened in his life. Job 13:15a says, *Though he slay me, yet will I trust in him.*

Now, that's trust. Job was saying that nothing could cause him to stop trusting God, not even death. He was saying that no storm in life could diminish his trust. Can you imagine how it made God feel when He heard Job say that?

Job made a choice to trust. Even though his world was falling apart around him, and even though he had no idea why it was happening, he still made the choice to trust God. Job's choice to trust had true impact. It brought glory to God when he said those words and even today, thousands of years later as we read them, it still brings glory to God. That is a Christ-like trust.

So choose to trust. Say, "It doesn't matter how bad circumstances are looking right now. It doesn't matter how frightened I am right now. It doesn't matter how much I'm hurting. It doesn't matter how confused I am. I know my God. I know He is always faithful, even when I can't see it and I don't feel it. So I choose to trust Him."

Remember to Trust

Another way to develop trust is to take the time to remind yourself of what God has done for you in the past. Do it often. Remember past blessings and past incidences where God has proven Himself faithful. It is easier to trust when you remember all God has done for you in the past. Remember all the times He has come through for you. Remember that He has never failed you.

Remembering God's blessings and faithfulness is important to trust. Remembering past blessings gives strength and courage to face the future with trust. It builds your faith muscles.

It is too easy to forget what God has done for you. I know that. I can be sailing along one day, confident that God is in control. Then something bad happens in my life the next day and my trust flies out the window. I quickly forget what He did for me yesterday. I panic. I start to fret and stew. But I have found that if I slow down long enough to remember what I know to be true about God, then trust begins to kick in. I can get a grip. Just remembering how faithful God has been in the past calms me and helps me to trust Him for what I face ahead of me.

It is a good thing to take the time to remember on a daily basis. Just as you take the time to choose to trust daily, also take the time to remember times in the past when God has been faithful to you. As you go through life, if you can turn around and look back to all God has done for you and everywhere God has led you, then it is so much easier to trust Him with the things that lie ahead.

I love the verse in Joshua where he reminds the people of Israel that God never failed to do one single thing that He promised He would do.

Joshua 23:14 says, *And, behold, this day I am going the way of all the earth: and ye know in all your hearts and in all your souls, that not one thing hath failed of all the good things which the LORD your God spake concerning you; all are come to pass unto you, and not one thing hath failed thereof.*

I heard a pastor's wife speak years ago. I don't remember anything she said except this one phrase: *God is in control and knows what's best for me.* I wrote that simple phrase down on a piece of paper. It became my motto. I knew I needed help learning to let God be in control. I needed help learning to trust Him to do what was best for me. So I repeated that phrase over and over.

It did help. Now, whenever a storm starts to brew, that is one of the first things that pops into my head. It helps me to trust God.

Remembering God's Word is so important to my ability to trust, I have a little business card holder that sits on my desk in easy view. It holds little cards on which I have written Bible verses that contain truths I need to remember. I often shuffle through those cards and read them. They give me strength. They help to build my trust. They help me to be more Christ-like.

I would recommend that you find a way to remember God's past blessings also. Our memories are short, so keep a blessings book. Or write down special Bible verses and blessings on 3x5 cards and keep them in a box where you can thumb through them on a regular basis. Or get a clear business card holder and cut card stock to fit into it. Write down verses that help you. Write down answers to prayer.

Just do whatever works best for you. Choose to trust because God is trustworthy!

CALMING YOUR STORM

I challenge you to take a closer look at your trustworthy God. Convince yourself from God's Word that you can indeed trust God.

- Find verses that talk about God's character. What kind of God do you serve? What is God really like? How can you begin to develop similar character traits? God tells us quite a bit about who He is in the Bible. He isn't hiding a thing. Take the time to get to know what kind of a God you serve. Especially study the verses that talk about why you can trust God and what happens when you do place your complete trust in Him.

- Find verses that tell you about God's promises. Often the verses on trust come with a promise. What are some of those promises? As you search the Scriptures, ask God to help you to fully understand, accept, and assimilate the things you learn regarding trust in Him.

- Take time to memorize the verses you find that help you specifically to build trust in God. You will find that just when you need to trust God, those verses will pop into your mind. They will help you to cling to your trust in God when the winds are blowing and the waves are crashing all around you. They become an anchor for your soul.

• Do you have a plan for facing storms that includes God? Whether you can see a storm brewing or are already in the midst of a storm, you can make a pact with God to give your storms into His control. Talk to God about your storms. Ask Him what you should do and not do. Wait on Him to show you the answer.

• Choose to trust daily. Tell God that today you want to trust Him. Ask for His help. Then remember to trust. Set up memorials like note cards that you can flip through and reread daily. Write down the ways God has proven Himself trustworthy in your life. Write down verses on trust. There are great hymns of the faith that will help you to remember to trust too. Sing or hum songs like "A Mighty Fortress," "Trust and Obey," "Day by Day," "All The Way My Savior Leads Me," "Hiding In Thee," "It Is Well," "He Leadeth Me," "Master The Tempest Is Raging," "Great Is Thy Faithfulness," and there are so many more. The words of these great hymns remind us to trust also.

• Take the time to ask God to increase your trust in Him. Daily talk to God about the storms in your life. Ask God to help you with the areas where you have the hardest time trusting. Then, instead of carrying all your burdens and fears away with you, leave them with God in perfect trust. It may take time to get so that you can do that, but keep at it!

MEMORIZE THESE VERSES

Proverbs 3:5-6 *Trust in the LORD with all thine heart; and lean not unto thine own understanding.*
In all thy ways acknowledge him, and he shall direct thy paths.
Psalm 56:3 *What time I am afraid, I will trust in thee.*

Courage in the Storm

CULTIVATE COURAGE

Some people just naturally have more courage than others. Or at least they act like they do. I'm one of those people who doesn't. I admit it. I'm a wimp. Courage doesn't come naturally to me.

For me, Plan A would be to totally avoid every storm in life. If that wasn't possible, then Plan B would be to get the storm over and done with as quickly and as painlessly as possible!

But over the years I have learned a curious thing. I have learned it would be foolish for me to think that living a storm-free life would be best for me. I only fool myself if I think that is the case. And I have learned the folly of not being honest with myself.

Without storms, we wouldn't need courage. We could live in our safe little world with a false sense of security. But it would be just that. False, because there are storms in life. There are things that demand courage. No one ever lives a storm-free life. Life is full of storms, so we need all the courage we can muster. And God expects us to cultivate courage.

The storms in life are crucial to teaching us important lessons we need to know in order to most effectively serve and honor God. One lesson God knows we need to learn is about courage. And amazingly, storms can build courage. Sure, they can terrify us. They can even bring the worst out in us at times. But if we obey God's commands, we'll pluck up our courage and we'll see that storms build our faith and cause us to be stronger and better able to serve God.

Courage is the next step after trust. It's putting your trust in God into action. First you trust that God will be faithful, then you follow up by facing your circumstances, or your fears, or whatever storm you encounter with courage.

GOD GIVEN COURAGE

I was an extremely shy and introverted teenager. I did my best to blend into the background, especially at school. Not many people noticed me and that was exactly the way I wanted it.

During my freshman year in high school, whenever a teacher would assign a speech or a written report, I always opted for the written report. Often the other students would get up and breeze through a speech they had spent a minimum of time preparing by throwing in a few facts amidst a flurry of words.

In the meantime I slaved away in the library for days researching in order to write a paper just so I wouldn't have to stand in front of the class to speak. But that was fine with me. I admired my brave classmates for having the courage to give a speech but I just couldn't bring myself to do the same. The thought of speaking before all those people just terrified me. I'd much rather do the extra work than humiliate myself by giving a speech.

When I started my sophomore year, my English teacher recommended that I take a college prep English class. When I did, I no longer had the option of not doing a speech assignment. It was mandatory if I hoped to stay in the class and keep up my grades.

Our first speaking assignment was a demonstration speech. I can't begin to tell you the anguish I went through. It's a fact that most people dread public speaking, but I think I was far more frightened than most people.

For weeks before my first speech was due I would get sick to my stomach whenever I even thought of the speech. When the day of the speech came I seriously considered staying home and saying I was sick. That wouldn't exactly have been a lie. I truly was ill with worry, but I knew staying home would just be putting off the inevitable.

I had chosen to demonstrate how to assemble a Christmas ornament. Not a wise choice. I can still picture the scene as plain as day. I began my demonstration. As I reached down to pick up the Styrofoam ball, my hands were visibly shaking. That embarrassed and unnerved me. I hadn't thought about the fact that I would look so nervous. Up to that point I had only worried about the fact that I might make a fool of myself with the things I said. As I looked at my hands, I realized that I didn't just sound foolish, I looked foolish too!

Then things got worse. My voice joined into the conspiracy. My voice and hands were shaking so hard that no one in class could possibly miss it. In fact, I doubt if anyone could breathe while I was up there. I had a hard time picking up the small glittery things that were supposed to be attached to the ball. I shook so hard that I could barely get near the ball I was holding with one hand to spear it with the pin in the other hand. It was fortunate no one got hurt!

To my credit, I stuck it out. I considered abandoning the whole speech and sitting down, but I knew I would have to add "acts like a foolish chicken" to the list if I did that. So I persevered to the bitter end.

As I slunk back to my seat I was mortified. So was everyone else in the room. I had originally been afraid that my classmates would laugh at me, but I needn't have worried. I made everyone so terribly uncomfortable that they didn't even think of laughing. Even the cool guys who sat in back, and made a practice of making fun of just about everyone, didn't make a sound. I'm sure the entire class breathed a deep sigh of relief and were just thankful that I had finally finished.

Afterwards, the teacher let me escape to the rest room. I cried because I was so embarrassed. Then I cried even harder when I remembered that I still had several more speeches to deliver that year.

Every speech after that was pure terror. It just got worse. I got to the point where I was afraid of being afraid. I became physically ill. I can't explain to you how frightened I was of giving a speech. I'm surprised my classmates didn't circulate a petition to ask that I not be required to give any more speeches.

In my senior year my best friend wanted me to take a speech class with her as an elective. It would be the only way we could have a class together that year. I looked at my dear friend as if she had gone insane and flatly refused. She didn't make that suggestion again. I knew I would never get over my terror of public speaking. There was no way I would willingly stand before a group of people and humiliate myself ever again. That was for sure!

So how did the teen who was so terrified of speech in high school end up majoring in Interpretative Speech at Bob Jones University, conducting Speech Seminars, and writing a bunch of speech text books? My only answer is that God gave me the courage to do what He wanted me to do. But it took my being willing to do all those things when God asked me to. I had to pluck up my courage.

After high school I didn't want to go away to college. The thought just didn't appeal to me. Instead, I followed my friend to a cosmetology school in Ann Arbor. It was during that time that Gary and I began to date. Gary was already an evangelist. He had been on the road for several years, but for a short period he was off the road and back at our home church. While he was there he was in charge of Junior Church.

When Gary asked me to help him with the puppet ministry I thought it would be fun. That was something I would enjoy doing. After all, I could hide behind the puppet stage and I would disguise my voice. Gary would stand out front and talk with the puppet. No one would see me. I could do that.

But after a few weeks Gary asked if we could switch places. He is a truly gifted puppeteer and he wanted to get behind the stage to do his magic. So he asked me to stand out front and talk to the puppet. I would have said no to anyone else, but I wanted to impress Gary. I was kind of sweet on him. So I said, "Yes," and found that standing in front of children wasn't so frightening. In fact, I found I was quite relaxed doing so. The puppet made me laugh and I enjoyed working with the children.

Eventually things became serious with Gary and me and we were married. I don't think I impressed him with my many talents. He says he was impressed that I was trying to cultivate interest in the things that were important to him. I chalk it up to the "love is blind" theory.

The wedding was on a Saturday night and we started meetings in a nearby church the next day. We didn't go on our honeymoon until two weeks after we had been married. As we walked from the trailer to the church that first Sunday morning, I pleaded with Gary not to tell anyone that we'd only been married for 14 hours! You shouldn't have to look at your watch when answering someone about how long you've been married!

From that first Sunday of our marriage I worked along side of Gary. I talked to the puppets and learned to assist with Gary's Gospel magic tricks.

One day, after we had been traveling for about a year, we were in a large church for a week of meetings. I was sitting on the front row waiting for my turn to go up and talk to the puppet. The pastor was seated next to me. Just before I stood to go up onto the platform, he leaned over and said to me, "We have a pretty good crowd tonight. There are about six hundred people here."

Mercy! I looked at him in astonishment. It was in that instant I realized I was doing the very thing I had always believed I could never do. I was standing in front of people - lots of people - and I was speaking. And I was enjoying it!

I was truly amazed. The Lord had given me the courage to do what He wanted me to do. The courage to do what had previously terrified me.

It didn't take me long after that to realize I needed some formal training if I were to minister effectively with Gary. I knew I needed to go to Bible college and I knew I needed speech training. And do you know, strange as it may seem, the Lord placed within my heart a deep desire to do just that. I wanted to major in speech.

The Lord opened the door for me to go to school and I plucked up the courage to step through that door. Gary continued to travel for two to three weeks each month while Rynda was enrolled in the elementary school on campus and I went to learn about speech. And the more I studied speech, the more I loved it.

Looking back, I think now I see the reason God allowed me to be so frightened of speech. When I started studying speech in college, I still had to learn to get over my fear. Speech did not come naturally to me, not the standing up to do it part and not the sounding good while I was doing it part. I noticed that many of my fellow classmates who were majoring in speech just seemed to naturally understand how to deliver a piece of literature or how to make a public speech sound right.

I didn't have any of that natural ability. Speech was hard work for me and I often had no clue about how to deliver a speech in such a way that the teacher would be happy with what I had done.

In order to survive, I began going to my speech teachers' offices and asking them for extra help. I asked what they were looking for in a speech. I asked them to explain speaking techniques.

I also began to carefully watch the other students. I made a point of noticing how the more experienced speakers stood and held themselves and delivered their lines. I listened to where they placed emphasis and how they used gestures, facial expressions, and vocal variety to support what they were saying. I watched confident speakers and saw how they acted before and during a speech. I also made note of those who didn't do such a good job.

In short, I picked apart each performance. Then I tried to imitate the good speakers. If the teacher gave me a good grade and praised my performance, then I knew I was on the right track. If not, then I watched some more and tried again.

By the time I was graduated, I had learned more than just how to stand up and give a speech. I knew speech forwards and backwards. I knew what made a good speaker. I knew effective techniques for speaking. I knew how to sidetrack stage fright before a performance. I knew how to tell others what to do also.

I believe God had a very specific purpose for letting me start out by being so frightened and so naturally awkward at public speaking. There was a reason I had to fight every inch of the way to get my degree. I believe it was because, when the time came that God showed me He wanted me to conduct Speech Seminars and to write speech text books, He had perfectly prepared me. He not only prepared me as a speaker, he had prepared me as an instructor. Isn't God amazing?

All of that to say, I'm a chicken. But I have found that even a chicken can have the courage it takes to do what God asks. And when you take that first step of faith to exercise your courage, then God steps in and does the rest. He gives the strength to do the job.

A Job To Do

God often tells us in the Bible to have courage. It's a job God gives us to do. So much of the rest of the Christian life is really God's job. He does the saving. He does the spiritual work in our hearts. He gives spiritual growth. He produces spiritual fruit. It's all Him. We can do so little on our own.

But God does give us a few jobs in the Christian life. One of those jobs is to cultivate courage.

God knows we will face situations where we must stand up to the unknown. He knows there will be days we have to face things that frighten us. He knows there will be times when the tempter comes to confuse and confound us. He knows that the storms of life will seem overwhelming to us.

He knows. So He tells us to have courage. And He understands that courage is not always an easy thing to come by. He knows that we don't feel like we have the courage to face the storms in our life. He knows that even when we don't completely succeed in putting on a brave face, at least we tried. And I think it pleases God when He sees that we are doing our very best to obey Him.

God even promises to aid us as we do our job. When we take a step of courage, then God extends His strength to us.

Psalm 27:14 says, *Wait on the LORD: be of good courage, and he shall strengthen thine heart: wait, I say, on the LORD.*

Isaiah 41:10 says, *Fear thou not; for I am with thee: be not dismayed; for I am thy God: I will strengthen thee; yea, I will help thee; yea, I will uphold thee with the right hand of my righteousness.*

God doesn't leave us alone to flounder around on our own. That is one reason He sent the Holy Spirit to live within us. The Spirit comes along side to encourage us when we just don't seem to have any courage of our own.

Romans 8:26 says, *Likewise the Spirit also helpeth our infirmities.*

1 Corinthians 12:7 says, *But the manifestation of the Spirit is given to every man to profit withal.*

When you are teaching a little one to do a job, first you show them how to do the job. They may be unconvinced that they can do the job, so you stand beside them and lend a helping hand as they put forth their best effort. Then you beam with pleasure and offer praise that they have done such a good job just to please you.

God is like that. Even though He assigns us the job of having courage, He doesn't turn His back and go tend to other things. Instead His Spirit stays close at hand. He leans over to watch. When a helping hand is needed, He reaches out in love and gives the help we need. Then He rewards us for a job well done because it warms His heart that we have tried to please Him.

Just as a parent knows that a child learning a new skill will not always do a perfect job, it is the effort, not a perfectly performed job, that brings a nod of approval. A parent knows the child will improve with practice. So God knows that while we may be doing our best to be courageous, there will be times when our courage is imperfect. But in love, He gives the extra help we need knowing that with His strength we will grow to become more and more courageous.

BLIND-SIDED

Late on the night of July 19, 1999, we drove Rynda from the hospital back to her apartment to gather a few items that she would need for the night. It would be the first of many nights that she would sleep on the chair next to Bo's bed. Every night that Bo slept at the hospital, Rynda was there beside him. Over the next four years they spent many hundreds of nights in the hospital.

When we got to the apartment she gathered hair items, a T-shirt, toiletries. She took the dog out for a run. Then, when she came back into the apartment, she sagged against the wall and closed her eyes. An anguished look washed over her features. It broke my heart and I will never forget it. It was the first moment she had allowed herself to think about all that the doctors had said about the leukemia. She had kept up a brave face all afternoon for Bo's sake.

"Last night everything seemed so normal!" Rynda whispered as a tear rolled down her cheek. "I don't think I can do this. I'm not strong enough."

In that instant I realized what pain and suffering both Bo and Rynda would have to endure in the days to come. That alone was enough to bring pain to my heart. It's a parent's worst nightmare. You desperately want to fix things. You want to kiss it and make it better. But you can't.

I looked over at Gary as he sat in the living room and saw that he had his glasses in his hands and he was weeping. No. This would not be easy for any of us. We were all afraid and hurting more than we ever had before.

Later, in the car as we headed back to the hospital, Gary and I tried to encourage Rynda. She nodded in agreement as the look on her face told us she certainly hoped we were right. She was trying her best to gather her courage.

"Yes, you can do this." Gary encouraged her. "God will give you the strength and courage you need."

And amazingly, He did. Throughout the next four years both Bo and Rynda displayed more strength and courage than I had ever imagined they could.

Drawing On God's Strength

That first night in Bo and Rynda's apartment I remember wondering how on earth Rynda was going to face life in the hospital? How was she going to face cancer?

We said comforting words. Words we wanted to believe. We assured her that God would give her the courage she needed. We weren't sure how that was going to happen, but He did! He gave her the strength and courage to do what she needed to do when she needed to do it.

One thing that concerned me was the fact that Rynda has always been afraid and sickened by the sight of blood. She is just like her dad in that manner. The sight of blood makes both of them pass out. So do needles.

When Rynda was in the seventh grade I took her to a clinic for a blood test she needed. The nurse pricked the end of one of her fingers and away we went, out to the lobby to pay the bill. As I was standing at the checkout counter writing a check with one hand and holding our coats and all of Rynda's school books with the other, I felt Rynda lean against me.

I turned to ask her to please not lean on me since I already had my hands full. I looked at her just in time to watch her sink to the floor in a dead faint. She had passed out from a tiny pin prick on the end of one finger!

Another time she almost passed out when a pastor friend happily described how he had once had a building crush his finger. We were all laughing as the pastor embellished the story from his past. I happened to glance at Rynda and I noticed that instead of laughing she was sitting there quietly, white as a sheet. She had become so ill from just listening to the story that she had to go into another room and lie down for about an hour to keep from passing out.

So I worried about how Rynda would take to life in the hospital surrounded by nurses and needles and blood. I worried they might end up with two patients on their hands. I wasn't so sure even God could take care of this problem.

When Bo first went into the hospital, his doctor decided he needed a port installed in his chest. They wanted to use it for administering medications, drawing blood, and giving chemo. During the installation surgery one of his lungs was accidently nicked but the surgeon didn't realize it. Later in his room it became evident to Rynda that something was wrong. She

The Eye of the Storm

called the nurse and they discovered his lung had collapsed. Rynda calmly did what she could to help as they prepared to rush Bo back to surgery.

On another occasion, Rynda noticed that the tube draining fluids from his lung was draining blood. She called the nurse and held Bo's hand while they determined what needed to be done.

When Bo was released to go home, Rynda handled cleaning and caring for his port with the ominous words of warning in her mind that it was extremely important that not even a single germ be allowed into the port because it would directly enter his bloodstream. It could cause a terrible infection. It could even be fatal.

I wouldn't have had the nerve to touch that port, but she cleaned and sterilized it daily for many months until they removed it. That took courage.

One time after Bo had come out of a period of remission, the doctors decided to try a new type of chemo. It was a very aggressive type and they warned the kids of the adverse affects. It was frightening to wonder what would happen. The evening before the chemo was to be administered, Rynda called and said to me, "Mom, do you remember when I was little and on Christmas Eve you would tell me, 'The sooner you go to bed, the sooner it will be morning?' Well, if I don't go to bed tonight, does that mean morning will never come?"

It took courage to get out of bed some mornings.

Gary and I often spent time at the hospital when Bo was there. We would sit with Bo and visit, or go to give Rynda a break, or go to take a meal. But we weren't there every day. We had to work but, truthfully, I also couldn't handle watching Bo suffer so constantly. I needed a break. But Rynda rarely left his side. That took courage.

During his many bone marrow biopsies, Rynda would rub Bo's hand and talk to him in an effort to distract him from the extremely painful procedure that he was enduring. She didn't leave the room or even turn away to not watch. She just kept up a lively conversation with Bo.

Rynda became Bo's eyes and ears. So often Bo was heavily sedated. So Rynda kept a running log of which doctor had stopped in, what had been said, and what tests were scheduled. When necessary she recorded his intake of fluids and their exit as well. She kept a close eye on the medications he was given and made sure that what the doctor had said should be done was being done. She did this daily.

When Bo was home, she cared for him more tenderly than any nurse could. She watched for the dreaded signs that the time had come to reenter the hospital. She worried that she wasn't always doing the right things. But she always did her best.

When Bo was in the hospital Rynda was only able to get to work now and then, but the Lord blessed her with a very understanding boss. When Bo was home, both Bo and Rynda tried to keep working at their jobs. They both must have been exhausted much of the time, but they worked hard to keep life as normal as possible.

Neither one of them wanted to know what was coming next. They didn't want to know what stage the cancer was at. The nurses gave them a handful of books on leukemia and later on the lymphoma he contracted from one of his rounds of chemo. Rynda handed the books to me and said, "Here, Mom. If there's something there we really need to know, then tell us. Otherwise we don't want to be sitting around just waiting for the next thing to happen." Then they continued to live bravely. Courageously.

I remember one day, just five days before Bo passed away, sitting by Bo's bed and watching while Rynda tried to keep Bo distracted as a nurse tried to find a vein to stick the needle in so she could give him some kind of medication. The nurse was having a hard time and had to try several times before she could find a vein that didn't collapse. I watched Rynda as she talked with Bo and did her best to keep his mind on her and off of the pain. I marveled that this was the girl who, at one point in her life, could not even stand to hear a funny story about a crushed finger. Here she was, bravely comforting her husband, as he was greatly suffering.

And Bo showed such courage too. He never complained. In the four years that he fought the cancer, I only remember hearing words of cheer, and kindness, and courage coming from him. He was always upbeat. He was thankful. He smiled and joked when he was up to it. Even when he was extremely ill he took the time and effort to smile and speak to those around him even though he obviously felt just plain terrible.

I am sure that in the privacy of his own home he had times of deep discouragement. I am sure fear gripped his heart now and then. But courage is not the lack of fear. It is pushing bravely ahead in spite of the fear. It is being strong even when you don't feel strong. It is continuing to put one foot in front of the other and to just keep going. It is facing the enemy and trusting the Savior to give you the strength to do what must be done.

Another Storm

Another thing that can cause courage to fail is the financial problems that often arise as a result of our storms. An illness can cause a huge financial storm. The cost of a hospital stay is amazing, and not in a good way.

The bill for the first couple of weeks that Bo was in the hospital came to over $45,000.00. There were times when the stays were longer and the bills climbed way over $100,000.00.

It is staggering to look at that amount and know you will be required to pay the deductible plus twenty percent at the very least. Then, add to that the doctor's bills, the medications, and the outpatient trips to the Cancer Center for biopsies and chemo treatments. And don't forget the monthly premiums on the insurance itself. It can be staggering! It was a fearful thing. I'm sure Bo and Rynda dreaded going to the mailbox.

There were times when Rynda called me on the phone crying. She would tell me what the latest bill was. It even frightened me. I couldn't imagine how long it would take them to pay off all those bills. It made my insides feel like Jello, and they weren't my bills!

I would say to them, "God will supply it somehow. Just have faith." Then I would hang up and fall on my face in prayer. "Lord, how on earth are they going to pay those bills? How can I tell her to have faith? Do I really mean that, or am I just saying some nice words to try to comfort her? Am I trying to put a band-aid on a gaping wound? Help them, Lord!"

Bo's medicines were costly. I went with Rynda to the pharmacy once and she asked the Pharmacist to give her a two day supply.

"Why not get the whole prescription at once?" I questioned. Rynda told me how much a month's supply cost. Then I understood. They often got their meds one day at a time while trusting God to supply what they needed for the next day when the next day came.

When Bo's doctor recommended that they fly to the MD Anderson Cancer Center in Texas for special cancer treatments, that added a whole other set of bills to the mix. MD Anderson insisted on their money, in cash, up front for Bo's first visit. And don't forget the airline tickets, meals, and hotel bills.

Courage can fail you so easily. But hang on to the trust that we talked about in the last chapter. It can give you the ability to face the scary times with courage. It can help you to believe that, against all odds, God will provide. It gives you the faith to believe God will go through every trial right beside you. He gives you courage when you need it. He provides what you need, as you need it.

God was so faithful to Bo and Rynda. Twice the kids were given a grant from the hospital that covered all the hospital bills which weren't covered by their insurance. Our friends and family also gave. Their church family was so generous in more ways than I can begin to describe. Somehow, they made it. There were still huge medical and funeral bills when Bo died, but eventually the Lord provided for all of those bills as well. It was nothing short of a miracle the way the Lord provided.

Through it all, the Lord was teaching us all to trust Him and to have courage. I mentioned in an earlier chapter that even though the financial storms Gary and I were experiencing were of our own making, I came to believe God still had a purpose that connected to Bo and Rynda. We were not able to help the kids too much, beyond buying some food and drugs for them. As a result they had to have the courage to trust that God would provide, not Mom and Dad.

If Gary and I had been able, we would have taken out loans and maxed out every credit card we had to help pay bills and later to help pay for a bone marrow transplant which he was never able to afford and insurance wouldn't cover. If the Lord had allowed us to have been financially secure, we would have given the kids every penny we had. But we had no money. So, instead of trusting in Mom and Dad's money, they trusted their Heavenly Father. And not once did He let them down.

Let me tell you, it increases trust and courage when you see God do the impossible! But even before the final outcome of those tremendous bills was known, Bo and Rynda plucked up their courage and decided to trust God to provide for them. One day Bo said to Gary and me, "It would be real nice if someone gave me $50,000.00, but when I need $50.00, God gives me $50.00!"

Courage Is Contagious

When you turn to those around you with words of courage about how God is strengthening you, you will find that it will help them with their storms also. Courage is contagious. You can pass it on.

Isaiah 41:6 says, *They helped every one his neighbour; and every one said to his brother, Be of good courage.*

Bo had learned courage along the way. And his courage came from God. It came from seeing God work daily on his behalf. It came from seeing that God never failed him. And by voicing his courage, he was passing it on to everyone around him.

Bo decided to face his fight with cancer with courage. He decided to face his financial needs with courage. And I cannot tell you how many times his attitude helped me to be able to face it more courageously also.

When I saw how Bo determinedly hung on to his hope in God, then it made me think, "Dear Lord, if I ever face cancer, help me to keep in mind how Bo did it. I want others to look at my life and my testimony and be able to draw courage from the way I respond to life's trials, just like Bo."

His courage was an inspiration to me. It encouraged me to think about how I should face life's storms. And his courage was an inspiration to many others as well. It was contagious.

Your courage in life's storms can also be an inspiration to others to cause them to want to lean more on Christ and to draw closer to Him. That brings glory to God.

A Command And A Promise

One wonderful thing to remember about the Bible verses we read on courage is that whenever God gives you the command to have courage, He always follows the command with a promise. Always.

When God asks you to be courageous, He promises that if you will have courage, He will be right there to strengthen you.

Deuteronomy 31:6 says, *Be strong and of a good courage, fear not, nor be afraid of them: for the LORD thy God, he it is that doth go with thee; he will not fail thee, nor forsake thee.*

You can be positive that if you display courage, in spite of any fears you may have, then God will give you the strength to do whatever He asks you to do. That's a promise from God and God never breaks His promises. Don't take my word for it, take God's Word.

If you do your part, God will do His part. That's a promise.

Christ-Like Courage

Again, let's turn to see how Christ faced fear and trouble in His life.

Christ came to earth for the express purpose of dying on the cross for our sins. He was not impervious to pain and suffering when he took on the form of man. He knew what it was to have the type of trials and problems that we have. He knew what it was like to face life's storms. Yet, He was an example of courage. He did not turn away from the terrible task that lay ahead of Him on the cross and in the grave. He faced it with courage.

Hebrews 12:2 says, *Looking unto Jesus the author and finisher of our faith; who for the joy that was set before him endured the cross, despising the shame, and is set down at the right hand of the throne of God.*

It took courage to endure a terrible death on the cross. But much worse than we can imagine was the sin of all mankind that He bore for us. How much courage it took for Christ to know that His own Father would turn His back on Him. Yet He courageously did what He had to do. And He did it for you and me. He did it for the joy of knowing that His shed blood would provide us with forgiveness of sin and an eternity in Heaven.

We can draw great courage from Christ's example. And it is through Him that we draw our courage. His example is our inspiration.

Philippians 4:13 says, *I can do all things through Christ which strengtheneth me.*

After Bo went to glory, a friend from church sent Rynda an e-mail. Let me share a little of it with you.

I'm not sure I told you then, but it was a huge honor to be present with him during those final minutes of his earthly life. I will never forget it.

I believe Bo was a tremendous example of how a true Christian faces suffering and death. He taught me a lot about suffering. Every time I attempted to encourage him, he encouraged me. I believe it's Philippians 2 that speaks of Jesus as seeking no reputation and humbling himself as a servant and becoming obedient to the point of death, even the death on the cross.

At anytime Bo could have "cursed God and died," but instead he was committed to accept the "good and bad" and to trust his God "even though He might slay him." I believe Bo suffered for the cause of Christ just as much as if his life had been taken on the mission field or if he was persecuted for his faith in some other manner. He remained faithful, gentle, and longsuffering. I remember Pastor John and I prayed for him on the day before his passing, and afterwards Bo removed his oxygen mask and thanked us. Wow, what a godly man.

1 Chronicles 19:13 says, *Be of good courage, and let us behave ourselves valiantly for our people, and for the cities of our God: and let the LORD do that which is good in his sight.*

Bo behaved himself valiantly and the Lord used his courage to be an encouragement to the hearts and lives of those around him. That was a Christ-like quality.

It doesn't take a superhuman person to exercise courage. Not even a saint. It just takes a person who reads God's Word and determines to obey it. It takes a person who wants to be like Christ. When God says, "Be of good courage," then he plucks up his courage. And God always follows up by giving strength and the assurance of His presence.

Courage Equals Victory

Courage is essential to victory in the Christian life.

When God led the Children of Israel to the Promised Land the first time, they sent in twelve spies. The spies looked around and noted all the wonderful things about the land. But they also noticed the big, mean looking people. When they gave their report to the rest of Israel, all but two of them said, "Sure, the fruit is big, but so are the people! We can't just walk in there and tell them to leave. We'd better go back to Egypt!" They lacked courage. And because of it, they did not get the victory over their enemy and they did not get to claim all the blessings God had prepared for them. That honor would go to their children.

After forty years of wandering around in the desert, God brought the people back to the land. Several times, as Joshua prepared to lead the people into the land, God emphasized to Joshua that he needed to have courage. God knew that without courage, the Israelites would once again turn and flee in fear. Without courage they would not experience victory.

God told Joshua in Joshua 1:9, *Have not I commanded thee? Be strong and of a good courage; be not afraid, neither be thou dismayed: for the LORD thy God is with thee whithersoever thou goest.*

So the Children of Israel took courage. They went to face the enemy, not with swords and spears, but with the courage to simply walk around the enemy city and give a mighty shout when Joshua gave the word. Their courage gave them the victory that God intended them to gain.

The word courage means to show valor, bravery, boldness, confidence. It means to be stouthearted, stalwart, and strong. Probably not many of those words usually pop to mind when you think about yourself, yet God tells you, "Be of good courage." And if God says you can be of good courage, then you can. The victory will be yours.

Calming Your Storm

I challenge you to obey God's command to have courage.

• Find verses that talk about courage. Think about them. Pay close attention to the promises that God gives along with His commands to have courage. Take time to memorize the verses that talk about courage. Repeat them to yourself.

• Where is your greatest area of lack of courage? What makes you quake? What makes you want to turn tail and run? Tell God about it. Ask for His help as you try to have the courage to face your fears.

• God gives you the job of having courage. Take your job seriously. Work on courage one step at a time. You may not be able to face every fear that you have all at once. Instead, pick one fear. Ask God to help you to have the courage to face it. Think about how God is helping you in that area. Thank God for His help. Then tackle the next fear.

• Take the time to see the results when you have obeyed God and exercised courage. Have others been encouraged? Has it increased your faith and trust in God? Is it something that will help you in the future to draw courage again? Record those impressions in your heart and mind to draw on when you are faced with the need of courage again. Record them in a notebook so that you can reread them often.

• Courage makes you more Christ-like and builds your faith. Remember the victories that come because you obeyed God and had courage. Remember that courage starts with trust. You can't have the courage to obey God if you don't trust God to do what is right in your life.

• Remember that courage is contagious. Remember that courage is mandatory for victory. Demonstrate courage during the storms in your life and others will notice. Be sure to give God the glory. Encourage others to have courage also. Pray for them as they face their storms.

MEMORIZE THESE VERSES

Psalm 27:13-14 *I had fainted, unless I had believed to see the goodness of the LORD in the land of the living.*

Wait on the LORD: be of good courage, and he shall strengthen thine heart: wait, I say, on the LORD.

Peace in the Storm

One of the hardest things for me to obtain in my storm was peace. That and joy. It seemed that with the storm raging so loudly and so fiercely, there was no way to have peace. It just seemed impossible.

Just hearing the word "cancer" associated with someone I loved very much was like being punched in the stomach. It certainly knocked the wind out of me. It disrupted my peace.

I totally related to the prophet Jeremiah when he said in Jeremiah 9:1a, *Oh that my head were waters, and mine eyes a fountain of tears, that I might weep day and night.*

Instead of experiencing the peace of God, worry, fear, and sadness seemed to be my new companions. There was a gnawing in my stomach and a heaviness in my heart that didn't seem to go away. My mind buzzed with questions about what would happen and how life would change. Emotional pain like I had never before experienced seemed to lodge in my chest and wouldn't go away. My heart hurt, literally.

But of course, the Bible states that we can have the peace of God. Philippians 4:7 says, *And the peace of God, which passeth all understanding, shall keep your hearts and minds through Christ Jesus.*

God is trustworthy. God's Word is true. So obviously there had to be some way to come by this elusive thing called peace. So I set out to find it. I won't tell you that I ever got to the place where, when the doctor's reports got continually worse, I smiled gayly and said, "Well, isn't that nice!"

No. All worry and fear did not magically disappear. But the panic did. A deep concern and even a sadness at the events we faced remained, but God did give a peace. And God gave me something else also. He gave me a totally different perspective on life.

When lines in the Post Office were slow and the clerk would apologize for the wait, I was able to genuinely smile and tell her that it was no big deal. I became more patient. And feeling patient is a type of peace.

When there was something I could do to help someone, whether I knew them or not, it gave me pleasure to do that task. Reaching out to others gives peace.

You see, I began to see that life's little troubles aren't as big as I had once imagined they were. I began to see that the things I do for others and the work I do for the Lord is really the most important thing in life. I knew that when someone did an act of kindness for me or for my kids, it made life so much easier. It brought peace. I hoped that passing on kindness, as unto the Lord, would make someone else's life a bit easier also. I hoped it would add to their peace.

Peace became not as much a feeling as a knowledge that God is in control and I can trust Him. It was a process of allowing God to bring a calmness to my heart by allowing Him to tame the storm that raged within, even while the storm continued to rage without.

Slowly, God gave peace in my storm. God can give you peace in your storm also. You may not always understand how you can have peace in the storms of life, but you don't have to understand it to experience it.

The Caregiver

It is a strange experience for a child to become the care-giver for a parent. You never expect to be in a position of being strong for the one who was once strong for you. Becoming a care-giver for your parent creates its own set of trials.

For one thing, neither of you is thrilled about the situation. Parents usually resent the loss of their freedom. Who can blame them? It's hard for them to relinquish their independence. Likewise the child dislikes becoming the one in charge as well. The added responsibilities are a challenge that taxes their emotions and physical well-being.

On July 4th of 1999, just two weeks before we learned that Bo had leukemia, my mom had a heart attack. Because of numerous other health problems, the doctors decided that even though she had two 100 percent blockages in her heart, they would not operate. It would be too risky.

From that time on my mom became very limited in what she could do. She also began to fall frequently. She never broke a hip, but she did break a rib, she smashed in her face, she broke a finger, and she did other small bits of damage.

Then she had a stroke. That took away even more of her independence. She lost much more control in her left leg and she was very weak. She could get around the house in a limited manner with a walker, but soon she was relying almost completely on a motorized wheelchair.

Mom did not want to give up. She didn't want to be stuck at home. She was an outgoing person and she thrived on being with people, but after her stroke she rarely got out. Occasionally on Sunday mornings she would determine to go to church. She loved to get out and see others and hear the message. But by the time she would shower, eat, and dress, she would be so exhausted that she could not go. She would sit and watch a TV sermon, but it was discouraging for her.

Things continued to worsen for Mom. By the last year of her life she was completely confined to a wheelchair for mobility. She could lift herself in and out of the chair but that was all. Gary and I were almost completely off the road by this time. The Lord was slowing down the number of meetings we were scheduling and our speech materials began taking the majority of our time so we were able to remain close to home. I took over the cooking and cleaning for Mom. I was glad I could do something to help.

Mom hated it. She appreciated the fact that I was there to help, but she hated the fact that she could no longer move about and do all the things she loved to do. She hated the idea that Gary and I were not able to travel because of her, although we repeatedly assured her that the Lord had taken us off the road. It was not her doing.

Then, in 2001, Mom had another stroke and it was a bad one. The day started out well. It was a Friday afternoon and I had returned from picking green beans in my friend Kay's garden. Mom snapped beans while we discussed the menu for supper.

Mom was really upbeat. She had been doing well with the physical therapist who came three times a week. She had been learning how to once again do some of the things she had lost in the last stroke. The two of them spent a great deal of time working on using her walker and getting her into her shower again. She especially hated to have me give her a bath. She would cry when I bathed her because she felt so helpless and embarrassed.

We were happy and excited Mom was doing so much better. The day came when Mom decided she would get up early the next Sunday to get ready for church, which included taking her own shower. We were having a happy weekend.

At dinner time that Friday, she rolled her wheelchair to the table to eat with us rather than take a tray by her chair in the living room. The meal was great, especially the fresh beans Mom had snapped.

Then Mom asked me to take her into the bathroom. I rolled her in and left. She could maneuver well enough to do that on her own. After a bit I realized Mom hadn't called for help in getting back to the living room. So I went to peek in her room.

The sight that greeted me was frightening. There sat Mom in her wheelchair. Her back was to me, but I could see by the way she was slumped in the chair with her head laying to one side and one arm hanging limply over the edge of the chair that something was very wrong.

I rushed in and asked if she was OK. She replied that she was fine. But I knew for sure she wasn't fine. I asked if she could raise her arm or leg. She insisted she could, but neither her arm nor her leg on the left side were responding. She protested when I said I was going to call the ambulance, but I knew she was having another stroke.

When we got to the hospital, Mom was rushed into the emergency room and I was rushed into the billing department. As I filled out paperwork nearby, I could hear Mom in the other room persistently asking the nurses where I was. "Where's Wendy? Is Wendy here?" she kept frantically repeating.

I finally finished filling out papers and hurried to her side. She took one look at me, glared, and exclaimed, "Why did you bring me here? To torture me?"

With that, she turned her head away from me and refused to look at me or talk to me for the rest of the evening.

The nurse worked to find a vein that wouldn't collapse. She stuck Mom over and over trying to start the IV and I could tell it was painful. Boy, did I feel guilty. I really didn't think I could have done anything differently than I had, but Mom hated being in the hospital and she hated being stuck so many times in so many painful ways.

Mom spent the next two weeks in the hospital. By the time I returned the next morning she had forgotten her anger with me. She was in a lot of pain. That day, as we waited for an ambulance to take her to the larger hospital in Greenville for a test to help find the source of her pain, I tried to distract her by talking about everything I could think of. We talked about when I was about three years old and Mom had taught me the twenty-third Psalm and the one-hundredth Psalm. We quoted them both. And neither one of us forgot a word. We talked about so many things.

That turned out to be the last really good talk I had with Mom. She was in horrible pain, but we were both trying hard to ignore that fact.

The tests showed there was no real pain, but the section of Mom's brain that controlled that information had been damaged. It was telling Mom that the pain was real. They put Mom on some strong pain killers. When it didn't help, the doctor increased the dosage. At one point they gave her so much medication that it was almost two days before she could be roused from sleep.

Gary and I had begun the process of purchasing a home just days before Mom's final stroke. Since Mom was totally out of it, we rushed the few miles from the hospital to our new home and began to move in the few things we would need to begin life in our very first house. We slept on the floor for a few nights until a bed was delivered.

During the two weeks Mom was in the hospital, I would rush there every morning to be with her during the day and I tried to move into our house and sleep with what time was left.

One day I asked Mom if she wanted some Coke. She said yes and waited for me to get one for her. But the bright red Coke can was on the tray, just inches from her hand and clearly visible. She could have easily reached it. I said, "Mom, can you see the Coke?"

"No." she replied.

I went out into the hallway and her doctor was there. I told him what had happened. "Has Mom lost some of her sight?" I asked.

The doctor went to examine her eyes and returned to tell me she had lost her sight and it most likely wouldn't return. That broke my heart. I cried all the way home that day. I couldn't imagine Mom not being able to see ever again. But she never once mentioned to me that she couldn't see. She didn't seem to notice.

The next day, the doctor sent Mom home in an ambulance. She couldn't even be moved to a wheelchair anymore. They used a stretcher. Mom was happy to be going home. In fact, she was so happy, aided by her medications, that she made up a song about going home and sang it over and over to the ambulance attendants as they wheeled her out.

The doctor said there was nothing more they could do for her. The next step was hospice when needed. I'll never know why the doctor didn't just start hospice at that point.

At home, the first week things were workable. But I worried about how to get her to eat so she could take her medicines. She never seemed to feel like eating. She mentioned once that chicken from KFC sounded good, so Gary rushed right out and bought some for her. She ate one bite and said it tasted good but she didn't want any more.

I worried about how to get her to take her medications. She refused to take anything. She told me that she wasn't sick and didn't need medicine. She would refuse to swallow any medicine until the last dose had worn off and she was in such terrible pain that she would finally agree. Then she suffered for hours until the pills began to work. And on it went.

Was I doing the right thing? Should I force her to eat? Was I giving her the best care possible? Questions and fears swarmed my mind and troubled my heart.

Mom also seemed to be a bit confused about things. She could remember things like the fact that her physical therapist came on Tuesdays and Thursdays. Her short term memory was very good to a point. She remembered that we now lived in South Carolina, but one day when Gary and I went out to dinner, she asked if we had gone to eat in Ann Arbor, Michigan.

She would say amusing things without meaning to. Because Gary and I had traveled in evangelism for so many years, we ate out in people's homes almost every night. I didn't learn to cook until much later in my life. But I was a pretty good cook by this time. At least I thought I was. One day I was trying to coax Mom into eating something. Mom consented to eat a bite of whatever I had fixed for dinner that night. She looked at me in surprise and asked, "Who cooked this?" I told her that I had. Then I added, "What's the matter, don't you think I can cook?" Without missing a beat she said in all seriousness, "I KNOW you can't!"

Sometimes she would ask things that really threw me off balance. I'll never forget the day Mom asked where her mother was. I was taken back by that. My mom was almost eighty-five years old. When I told her that her mom had died long ago, she looked at me and asked, "My daddy too?" When I said yes, she cried as if they had died just the day before.

It broke my heart. The next time she asked, I told her, "They are resting." I figured that was truthful without being hurtful. It got so she would say, "Are Mother and Daddy resting?"

Mom continued to get worse and I suspect that she was continuing to have mini-strokes. Each day she seemed to get worse. I felt like she was getting sicker on my watch. What was I doing wrong? What was I to do?

I sat by her bedside and watched her even when she was asleep. Dad took night shifts, I took the day. I had a baby monitor that I kept in her room with the speaker on my desk in the office that I turned on when I had to do some work. It was so sensitive I could hear her breathe. One strange sound and I was running for the house.

Sometimes she would beg me to take off her shoes and socks because her feet hurt so badly. But I couldn't. She didn't have shoes or socks on! When the pain was so bad, I would try to distract her. But it got so that I couldn't. Then I would pray.

The Home Health Care nurse assured me things were as good as possible, but I wasn't so sure. Mom wasn't getting better. At the beginning of Mom's second week at home, I called Dr. Kendall, our family doctor. He's a wonderful Christian man who was so comforting to Mom when she used to go visit him for her regular doctor visits. If he didn't know what to do for her, he would bow his head and pray with her and ask God for wisdom. Mom found it very reassuring that her doctor would pray for her.

On an earlier occasion I had asked the doctor several questions and expressed my concern about whether I would know what to do for Mom. I'm sure I looked worried.

"Don't worry," he comforted me. "God will give you the wisdom you need."

So that morning, when I called Dr. Kendall, I explained what was happening. He asked, "Do you want to send her back to the hospital so they can feed her by IV?"

I dreaded that thought. Her veins were so weak and it was always such a painful thing for her.

"I don't know." I said. "I don't know what the right thing is anymore."

"Would she want to go back?" he asked.

"Oh, no. She hates it there," I replied.

"There's your answer. I'll arrange for hospice to start today," he said.

The Eye of the Storm

In came hospice. Finally I could breathe a sigh of relief. It didn't make Mom's situation too much better, but it took a huge burden off my heart. They helped bathe her. They put her on a narcotic patch which stopped the need for oral meds. Finally she was completely out of pain.

That first afternoon when the hospice people left, Mom looked at me and asked, "Wendy, am I dying?" I had no idea what I should say. Every time we had visited Dr.. Kendall in the past, she would jokingly ask that question. He always shot back, "Yes, but not today." So I gave her that reply as a gentle tease. But I wondered what I should have said. I think she must have thought that if she had hospice, then she must be dying.

The first time the hospice nurse gave Mom morphine I felt ill and almost vomited. How could this be happening? Soon Mom slipped into a deep sleep and almost never roused. One day our Compassionate Care Pastor came to visit. He stood by her bed but she wouldn't even open her eyes. She whispered, "Tell him I'll see him later. I need to sleep now."

I spent lots of time just sitting by Mom's side. She didn't wake to talk to me anymore, but I would watch her and pray. As I sat there the last two lines of a poem by Dylan Thomas kept going through my head.

> "Do not go gentle into that good night.
> Rage, Rage, Against the dying of the light."

I got so I hated those words. I was tired of raging. I wanted peace. So I made up my own words.

> "Go gentle into that good night.
> Sleep, sleep, sleep.
> Safe in the arms of Jesus.
> Safe in the Savior's keep."

I repeated those words over and over to myself. I was still deeply concerned, but as I allowed myself to dwell on the fact that Mom would soon be in Heaven with Him, a peace did come to my heart. I realized that all was in God's hands. And what safer hands could we be in during the storm?

On the following Sunday, at 7:30 a.m., Dad called me.

"Wendy, you better come quick. I think Mother is worse."

Gary and I flew the few miles that separated our homes. When we got to the door Dad pulled it open and said, "I think she's gone."

And she was. She had taken her final breath just moments before I got there. I was a bit taken back by that. I was surprised she had not waited for me before she died. But she was gone.

I sat beside Mom for over an hour while we waited for the hospice lady to arrive. I held her hand and talked to her the whole time. It was such a peaceful experience. She wasn't in pain. She was finally with the Lord. It was as happy of a time as it was sad.

The thing I remember most about taking care of my mother was the uncertainty about whether or not I was doing the right thing. It tormented me at times, both before and after Mom died.

During much of the same time I was caring for my mother in South Carolina, my sisters-in-law, Lois and Lee, were caring for Gary's dear mom in Michigan. Gary's mom lived with Lois until she passed away. Conversations with them let me know that I wasn't the only one that felt the way I was feeling at times. It was a comfort to know someone understood what I was going through.

Gary's mom passed away about five months before my mom and both Lois and Lee helped me with their kind and supportive words, both before and after my mom died. I still keep an e-mail from Lee that she sent the day after Mom died.

I learned that I was not God. I could not control circumstances. I could not know exactly what to do. But I had done my best and the Lord gave me the peace to accept that fact. He gave me the peace to realize that because He is in control, all things are done in His time and in His way. I could rest in that truth.

PEACE DISRUPTERS

I found that if I wished to have any true peace, I first needed to have peace with God. Then I could have peace with my storm. Be assured, you can't have peace in your storm if you don't first have peace with God. You must have peace with God to experience peace in your storm.

Turmoil from within my own heart and mind, as well as turmoil from outside sources, often did their best to destroy my peace. I call these peace disrupters.

Both internal and external disrupters can destroy peace. Sometimes you only face one disruption in life at a time, but that is rare. Normally one disrupter leads to another. And life comes at you from so many different angles. You often can't limit what disrupts you to one thing at a time.

An external peace disrupter can easily stir up several internal peace disrupters. Disrupters can come as a result of your own sin and foolishness, but they can just as easily come from no fault of your own. Let's look at a few peace disrupters and the effects they can have in your life. There are others not mentioned here. Ask the Lord to show you your peace disrupters.

Internal Disrupters

Anger

Anger destroys peace. No question. There is no way you can be angry with someone or something and still experience peace with God. It just isn't possible.

The Bible does talk about the Lord's being angry, but God's anger is always directed toward sin. Sometimes it was the sin of the heathen people but often it was caused by the sin of His own people. He loved the Children of Israel, but He was angry when they disobeyed. He wasn't angry for a selfish reason. He was angry because He knew what damage their sin would do to their relationship with Him. He was angry because He fully understood the destructiveness of sin. But more often than not, instead of anger, the Lord was quick to show mercy and compassion. When the people repented of their sin, the Lord was anxious and willing to forgive.

Psalm 145:8 says, *The LORD is gracious, and full of compassion; slow to anger, and of great mercy.*

But you and I aren't usually filled with righteous indignation. Our anger is usually petty and self-serving. We lash out without any thought of what damage it may do. When I first got married, I often got angry when I didn't get my way. I was young and childish. I had unrealistic ideals about life and marriage.

Most of my anger was directed at Gary. The poor man would ask what was wrong and I would reply, "Nothing." I would pout and refuse to talk to him. Or if I was really steamed, I'd let him know - fully - what the problem was. I'd explode in his face.

Fortunately, Gary is very patient and very wise. He didn't return my anger. Instead he calmly insisted that we talk things through. As much as I didn't want to talk, it did help to get things out in the open. Then I could simmer down and we could move on.

In time I began to realize that anger was becoming a normal reaction for me. It was just something I automatically did when things weren't perfect to my way of thinking. But I didn't like the way I was acting so I began to take the time to examine my anger from a different perspective. I realized I was wasting my time, energy, and happiness on my selfish need to have things my way. I was destroying my own peace and the peace in my home.

I realized that peace in our home was worth more than getting my own way. I realized how destructive it was to be angry at the one I loved so much. So I began to pray about my problem. I won't say it was quick or easy. It was hard to let go of my anger, but slowly, with the Lord's help, I began to let loose of it. And as the anger left, peace began to return, both to my heart and to our home.

Ecclesiastes 7:9 says, *Be not hasty in thy spirit to be angry: for anger resteth in the bosom of fools.*

I found that I could discuss an issue with Gary before I got angry and resolve it without all the drama. How much better that was! How much peace it brought to our home. How thankful I am that a foolish action can be replaced with a wise one.

Maybe you have a problem with anger. When things don't go your way, you let loose. And as a result, you don't have much peace. I won't tell you it was easy to change. It wasn't. It took several years to really get to the place where anger wasn't my automatic reaction. But I will tell you that anger can be overcome with prayer and work. And the results are worth all the time and effort.

Listen to what the wisest man on earth said about anger. Then let his words apply that wisdom to your heart.

Proverbs 15:18 says, *A wrathful man stirreth up strife: but he that is slow to anger appeaseth strife.*

Proverbs 16:32 says, *He that is slow to anger is better than the mighty; and he that ruleth his spirit than he that taketh a city.*

Maybe you have anger that is a result of the storm you are facing. You may be angry at God for allowing you to go through the storm. You may be angry that someone you love is going through a terrible storm. Sometimes it is easier to handle a problem yourself than it is to watch your loved ones suffer while you can do nothing to help. As a result, you are angry that your loved one must suffer while you are helpless to do anything.

We have all heard that we should never question God. We have been taught that we should never ask, "Why?" But I believe God would rather you bring your anger out into the open and discuss it with Him. It is better to do that than to bottle it up and pretend it doesn't exist in an attempt to appear spiritual.

I don't believe God is so delicate or quick to wrath that He will turn from you if you express your anger toward your storm and toward Him. You can be honest with God. He can take it.

Job's storm caused more grief and sorrow than many of us will ever experience. Job spoke to God about his bitterness. God did not rebuke him.

Job 7:11 says, *Therefore I will not refrain my mouth; I will speak in the anguish of my spirit; I will complain in the bitterness of my soul.*

Expressing anger is not wrong. What I do think is unhealthy is allowing your anger to turn into a deep, lasting bitterness that drives you away from God rather than turning you toward Him in your times of need. Don't let your anger separate you from the One who is your only true source of help in your time of storm. Express your anger if you need to, but then put your anger aside and turn to God to give you the peace you desperately need.

Hebrews 12:15 says, *Looking diligently lest any man fail of the grace of God; lest any root of bitterness springing up trouble you, and thereby many be defiled.*

Guilt

My angry outbursts caused me quite a bit of guilt. I never enjoyed my anger. I hated how I acted. After an outburst of anger, I would be totally ashamed of myself. I would beat myself up mentally for being so terrible. I had no peace.

I would tell myself how terrible I was. I would berate myself verbally to Gary. I quickly learned not to say how terrible I thought I was in front of Gary because it made my normally calm husband very angry. He would say, "Don't talk about yourself like that! I love you and I won't let you say things like that about the person I love."

The Lord gave me a kind, patient husband who wouldn't let me say bad things about myself. No matter what I did or said, he just kept loving me. Not every woman is that blessed, I know.

But I felt so guilty.

Guilt is a terrible feeling, but God gave us guilt for a reason. It can be a good thing. The Lord gave us guilt so we will know when we are in the wrong. Contrary to what most Psychologists say, there are things we should feel guilty about. Our sin should make us feel guilty. But sitting around and beating ourselves up about it isn't the answer. God gave guilt so we will take the needed action to put away our sin and get right with Him.

Then, when we have done that, we need to put aside our guilt. When we confess our sin, God will forgive. When we put our sin behind us and live the way He wants us to live, He says we have nothing to feel guilty about. When God forgives us, we are no longer under condemnation. Translation: We don't have to feel guilty anymore. We can have peace with God.

Romans 8:1 says, *There is therefore now no condemnation to them which are in Christ Jesus, who walk not after the flesh, but after the Spirit.*

I found that I had to forgive myself and I had to keep trying when I failed. Believe me, I failed quite often. But I learned that instead of saying, "See, I still get angry. I can't change." I would say, "Okay. I didn't handle that so well, but I'll keep trying. Next time I'll do better."

And eventually, I did. You will too.

Fear

If you haven't picked up on it by now, I will plainly admit that one of the biggest peace disrupters in my life is fear. It has always been that way. I don't know why. I have been afraid of so many things in my life. Fear of public speaking, fear of what others think of me, fear of doing something wrong, fear of just about everything. It's a feeling that's never far from me. My hand is never far from the panic button.

When I began to realize how much fear I harbored, I knew my fear showed a lack of trust and faith in God. It also robbed me of peace. I didn't have much peace when I was in a constant state of fearfulness. So I began to pray about it. I decided it would be my next spiritual project.

When I say "spiritual project," I mean something I need to work on in my life. I have found there are many things in my life I need to work on in order to be a better Christian. It's an ongoing process. But I found it overwhelming to list all my shortcomings and downfalls and try to correct them all at once. So I decided that I would work on one thing at a time. I would start with my main sin or obstacle to being an effective Christian and I would zero in on that. I would pray about it. I would look verses up that pertained to it. And I would really focus on correcting it.

Fear was one of the things that I chose as an early project. In fact, fear is so deeply imbedded in me that it continues to be an ongoing project. But I have learned many things about my fear and I've also learned many things about the peace that comes from eliminating fear.

Fear can cause you to do and say some very foolish things. It can cause you to blindly grasp for solutions to life's problems without first looking to God to give you the perfect solution.

John 14:27 says, *Peace I leave with you, my peace I give unto you: not as the world giveth, give I unto you. Let not your heart be troubled, neither let it be afraid.*

EXTERNAL DISRUPTERS

Okay, those are a few internal peace disrupters. Now let's look at some external disrupters.

People
You know that the people around you can greatly disrupt your peace. They can truly upset your heart and mind, not to mention your schedule! Here are just a few ways people can add to or even create storms in your life.

People Can Make Unfair Demands.
When people expect more of you than you can give or than you can do, it can become a problem. There is only so much of you to go around. There is only so much you can do in life.

It depends on who the person is and what they are demanding. Some people rightfully have a greater claim on you and your time and talents. Your family is important. Often people have time for everyone except their family. When Gary and I traveled we often saw that problem in ministry families. The Pastor was often so busy caring for his congregation that his family suffered. It was often true of the Pastor's wife also.

I used to have a hard time saying, "No." But when the Lord clearly showed me He had a specific job I needed to be doing for Him, then I began to realize that I would have to stop doing what everyone else wanted if I were to do what God wanted. It is with a peaceful spirit that I can turn down projects I know will cut into my time of doing what God wants me to do. What God wants for me must always come first. That's job one and if I have time for other things, fine. If not, then the other things must not be done.

Even good things can be wrong for you to do. Just because someone wants you to do something doesn't mean you should. So often we cram our lives full of things we don't even feel led of God to do. Why? Because we have a hard time saying no for fear of what others will think. We feel guilty when we say no. Often, our storms would calm if we could just slow down and put our priorities in order.

It is never a good thing to do something just because someone else thinks you should. Only you and God can determine what is best for you. You need to be in prayer about what you should be doing and about what should be expected of you.

It is never wrong to tell someone you need to pray about what God wants. Then do just that. Pray about it. If God does not give you peace, then you can say with a clear conscience, "I don't believe God wants me to do that now. I already have a full plate."

People Can Give You Guilt Trips.

When you deal with people who place unfair expectations or unfair demands on you, you may find that when you say, "No," they will try to make you feel guilty. Or maybe you just feel guilty anyway.

I mentioned that some guilt is good for you. Godly guilt over sin is good. But there is unhealthy guilt too. There is guilt that God never meant for you to bear. I'm talking about guilt that others put on you for not doing things their way. Their selfishness thrust on you should not bring you guilt, but often it does.

In a storm others can make you feel guilty by expecting things from you that you cannot do. They may want more of your time than you can give. They may want you to do something you know you can't do.

I have found that I have very little control over what others say and do in an attempt to make me feel guilty. I can't control them. I can't stop them. What I can do is to not let them make me feel guilty.

I know! I know! That's easier said than done. But again, it's something that needs to be a matter of prayer. If you have someone who places guilt on you for no fault of your own, then you need to ask the Lord to help you to release that guilt and put it behind you. Allow the Lord to control your feelings. Don't let people control your feelings.

People Can Be Unsympathetic or Antagonistic.
People aren't always sympathetic of your storm. When I was thinking about my kids and their problems, I often was not focusing on what was going on around me. There were times when I was quite distracted and absent-minded. I found that others often frowned on that. They didn't seem to care about my problems. That made me feel badly at times. It even angered me at times.

Then I realized that I wasn't the only one in life going through a storm. Others probably have enough problems of their own. Often others are in the midst of a raging storm themselves. Who can blame them for not wanting to confront your storms or be understanding of your storms?

Looking outward and offering sympathy and understanding to others helps to create peace in your heart. Those around you may not ask for your pity or even your help, but everyone appreciates a smile and a kind word.

When you don't seem to be getting the reaction you want from those around you, take the time to look outward at those people. Maybe they need a little of God's love shown to them. Maybe God is opening a door for you so you can bring glory to Him by showing godly love.

People Can Be Angry At You.
We talked about your anger towards God and towards others. But what about anger that is directed toward you?

Maybe you are not the one who has a problem with anger. Maybe you have to deal with someone near you who has that problem. One thing that dissolves anger quickly is a kind and forgiving spirit. Rather than meeting anger with anger, meet it with love and gentleness. You'll be amazed how effective that can be. It cooled my jets many times.

I think the way my husband responded to me when I was angry was quite effective and quite godly. After all, it is hard to argue with someone who is not willing to argue back.

The Bible says in Proverbs 15:1 *A soft answer turneth away wrath: but grievous words stir up anger.*

It certainly is a Christ-like response.

I Peter 21b-23 says, *Christ also suffered for us, leaving us an example, that ye should follow his steps:*

Who did no sin, neither was guile found in his mouth:

Who, when he was reviled, reviled not again; when he suffered, he threatened not; but committed himself to him that judgeth righteously.

Circumstances

There are a million circumstance that can come up to disrupt your life and steal your peace. Almost daily there will be unexpected things that cause you to be thrown into turmoil. Some circumstances you can control or fix. Some you cannot. Most often, you will not be able to control the changes in life that come your way.

Not many people like surprises, at least not the type of surprises that don't come in gift wrapped boxes. The surprises of life aren't always so welcome.

By now you know that I like to know what is going to happen in advance. To be more specific, I like to plan what is going to happen. I keep an organizer and I live by it. It's the first thing I reach for when I get to my desk. If I were to lose it, I might just as well not get out of bed in the morning!

I list what I need to do each day and check items off as they are accomplished. I write down appointments. I schedule meetings and shopping dates. I've even been known to schedule time to polish my toe nails. I guess I'm not a spontaneous type of person. I prefer that everything goes as scheduled in my organizer. After all, I'm not just writing things down to be using up ink!

I don't much like it when the unexpected throws a monkey wrench in my day let alone in my entire life. But amazingly enough, I have learned that sometimes the unexpected can be God's way of ordering my steps. I try to remind myself that my life is to be ordered by Him, not by my organizer.

Psalm 37:23 says, *The steps of a good man are ordered by the LORD.*

Often, what appears to be a storm to you is not so to God. What you see as an annoying inconvenience or even a raging storm may very well be God's way of ordering your steps. You need to be open to the fact that even though you are not in control of the circumstances of life, God is. He does not allow things to happen to you that are not in His plan.

Life does not take God by surprise. He is not thrown off balance by circumstances. God is not caught up in your traumas, not to say He isn't concerned or involved, He just isn't thrown by them. God does not sit in Heaven wringing His hands saying, "Oh, no! Did you see that? How could that happen? What will I do now?"

That knowledge brings peace. Even when the people or circumstances of life are out of your control, they are not out of God's control. Nothing disrupts God's control.

Problems With Disrupters

Disrupters cause agitation and agitation is the opposite of peace. The two do not co-exist. Agitation is loud, disconcerting, clamorous, deafening, and full of pandemonium. None of those qualities aid in peace.

Whether the agitation you experience comes from an internal disrupter or an external disrupter, it can still cause some very serious problems. Life's storms not only disrupt your mental and emotional peace of mind, they can greatly upset your physical well-being also.

A couple of weeks after Bo was diagnosed with cancer, I began to notice that my teeth ached. All of them. Sounds strange, but my entire mouth hurt. I couldn't imagine that all my teeth had gone bad at once, but I made a dentist appointment to see what he had to say. The dentist looked around carefully and took X-rays. He said he saw no problems out of the ordinary. Then he asked if there was anything stressful happening in my life. He said stress and tension could cause the pain. After I explained what was going on in my life, he gave me a knowing nod and recommended that I work on relaxing. He was right. When I took the time to consciously relax, the pain would go away.

During that same time my normally low blood pressure spiked to a dangerously high level and my shoulders began to ache all the time. Often I felt like crying, even when there didn't seem like any immediate problem was at hand. This went on for four years. My doctor tried several blood pressure medications, but none of them helped at all. He told me that when my life settled down, my blood pressure probably would too. He was right.

I can only imagine what Bo and Rynda were going through. Even when I didn't think I was feeling that much fear or stress, my body was saying something different. My fear and anxiety had taken over and my body was letting me know so loud and clear.

Lamentations 2:11a says *Mine eyes do fail with tears, my bowels are troubled, my liver is poured upon the earth.*

Other problems can also arise. Depression is a very real problem that often develops from the constant wearing away of your peace of mind and body. It's so easy to become discouraged and give way to depression.

Another major problem is sheer exhaustion. It can be very tiring to be out of your routine while at the same time trying to do all the normal things life demands such as laundry, cooking, caring for children, and other family needs. Adding in doctor appointments, hospital stays, and caring for someone who needs you can make life seem impossible. You can become exhausted quickly.

You may even be losing sleep because of the strange hours or responsibilities you have added. You may find yourself lying in bed staring at the ceiling while you should be sleeping. But sleep won't come. It doesn't take much to become worn out. And exhaustion often leads to depression and many other problems.

You can't eliminate all the stress that goes together to cause the physical problems I have mentioned, but there are certain things you can do to help.

Take time to listen to your body. Do you need a nap? Take one. Do you need to get to bed earlier than normal? Go to bed early. Do you just need a break? Make arrangements and then take some time to be alone. Read, drink a cup of tea, call a friend, pray and read your Bible. Do something that will refresh you. Carving out just a little quiet time is so important. It will go a long way toward helping you to continue doing what you need to do.

And don't forget to exercise. Even a fifteen minute walk can help you to have more energy and it's a great way to clear your mind. Exercise releases tension, lowers blood pressure, and helps both your mind and body to cope. I check out cassette books from our library to listen to while I walk on our treadmill. Humorous books are great. They make me forget my storm for awhile. Thirty minutes in the morning is a great stress reducer and it helps me sleep better at night.

You must realize that staying in the best physical condition possible is essential, especially if you are a caregiver. Often, if your problem is health related, then everything possible is being done to help the person who is sick. But the caregiver often finds that they are neglecting their own needs. They are concentrating so intently on the needs of another that they ignore their own needs.

This may seem noble, but in the long run, it can be harmful to everyone. The person with the problem needs the caregiver to stay healthy so they can continue giving care. If that doesn't happen there will be more trouble ahead for everyone.

God intends for you to care for your body and your mind. He wants to give you both physical and mental peace. Your body is the temple of the Holy Spirit. It is an important thing to God. Treat God's temple, your body, with respect.

Seek Peace

So how do you banish these peace disrupters that cause such an uproar in your life? I won't lie. It's not easy. Some of the disrupters, such as the circumstances you face and the people you must deal with, may remain as a permanent fixture in your life. You may not be able to banish all disrupters. You may need to find a way to make peace with them.

God tells us we should seek peace. That sounds like an action to me. Seeking peace is something constructive you can do when all else around you appears to be destructive.

The world talks about peace. They spend lots of time and money seeking peace, but they never truly find it. They certainly don't understand peace or it's source.

God talks about the wicked man's pursuit of peace in Isaiah 59:8, *The way of peace they know not; and there is no judgment in their goings: they have made them crooked paths: whosoever goeth therein shall not know peace.*

The source of peace is God. God alone. There is no peace outside of God. And God wants you to have peace. He says it so many times in the Bible.

Jeremiah 29:11 says, *For I know the thoughts that I think toward you, saith the LORD, thoughts of peace, and not of evil, to give you an expected end.*

God tells us in several verses that we are to seek peace. We are to pursue peace. We are to diligently follow after peace. So peace doesn't seem to be a passive thing you just happen to stumble upon. It is something you must spend time and effort to find and obtain.

Psalm 34:14 says, *Depart from evil, and do good; seek peace, and pursue it.*

2 Timothy 2:22 says, *Flee also youthful lusts: but follow righteousness, faith, charity, peace, with them that call on the Lord out of a pure heart.*

Hebrews 12:14 says, *Follow peace with all men, and holiness, without which no man shall see the Lord.*

1 Peter 3:11 says, *Let him eschew evil, and do good; let him seek peace, and ensue it.*

So how do you seek peace?

Seek peace by staying close to the One who gives peace. The closer you are to God, the more you experience His peace. When I take the time to go to God's Word, He speaks to me. When I take the time to pray, I can pour my heart out to Him and know He hears and He cares. Not only that, He can do something about my storm. It may not be what I want Him to do, but He will always do what is best. All of God's ways lead to peace. I can rest in that.

When you are close to God, you have the peace of a clean heart and life. Being close to God causes you to desire to please Him by obeying Him. Being close to God is the most wonderful place you can be. It is the place of peace.

> There is a place of quiet rest,
> Near to the heart of God,
> A place where sin cannot molest,
> Near to the Heart of God.

Near to the Heart of God by Cleland McAfee

I love the idea of being near to God's heart. The song speaks of an intimate closeness that I experience with few others. It reminds me of how much God loves me.

And God loves you too. God longs to gather you close to Himself. He longs to whisper words of calm and peace to you. The roar of the storm can deafen you to the still, small whisper of God's voice. But only if you let it.

God calls you to have peace by trusting in Him. He calls you to peace by obeying Him. Without trust and obedience there is no peace. But often the uproar of the storm causes you to quit listening to His voice. You stop doing what you know is the will of God for your life. You stop praying and reading His Word. You stop obeying His Word.

Be careful to listen for God's voice, even when you find yourself distracted by the storm that roars around you. Trust God to do what is right for you. Continue obeying despite the winds that blow. Knowing and doing God's will, as you know it from His Word, has a calming effect. It brings security and safety. It brings peace. Let your storm drive you closer to God. The closer you are to God, the easier it becomes to trust and obey Him.

No matter how long you have been a Christian, trusting God and obeying Him is still a day by day, moment by moment decision that you need to make. But one of the rewards of the closeness that comes from trusting and obeying is peace. And what a wonderful reward that is!

Isaiah 32:17 says, *And the work of righteousness shall be peace; and the effect of righteousness quietness and assurance for ever.*

The Bible also says in Isaiah 26:3 *Thou wilt keep him in perfect peace, whose mind is stayed on thee: because he trusteth in thee.*

Keep your mind on God. Think about Him and His Word. Dwell on what you know to be true about Him. God promises that when you keep your mind on Him you will have peace.

How true that is. When you remember how faithful God is and how He guides and protects, then you can have perfect peace. Even when events are not going the way you would choose, dwelling on God and drawing close to God helps you to remember that God does everything for your good and His glory.

The Snow Storm

One of the surest ways to obtain peace is to set your mind on the fact that God is always with you and He is always working for your good. If you can keep your eyes on your Heavenly Father then you can have peace, even when all else is in a total uproar. You can be safe and secure in your Father's presence.

Peace in the Storm

It was a cold, wintery day in southern Michigan. I pulled the covers up over my head and dreaded the thought of climbing out of my warm bed into the cold morning air. The furnace was running, but it barely kept back the frigid temperature that had turned the great outdoors into a deep freeze.

It was the first really big cold snap of the season and the weatherman had warned of a possible blizzard developing in the night. But a glance out the window showed only a few flakes coming down. There was no blizzard now, so I knew I would have to climb out of bed and get ready to go to class. A little snow never stopped anyone in Michigan.

I had finished high school the year before and still wasn't sure what I was going to do with my life. I didn't have peace about going to the Bible college that most of my friends from church had attended and I didn't know anything about any of the other Bible schools.

I did know I had to do something. My parents had given me one last summer to be with my friends, to swim and to just enjoy being young. But that had to end. When summer was over I had to make a decision, so when my best friend announced she was going to a cosmetology college to learn to be a beautician, I decided to try that. I wasn't that good at doing hair or even interested in doing that for a living, but I thought beauty school sounded like a good way to keep busy while I made up my mind about what I wanted to do with the rest of my life.

"Why couldn't that blizzard have come?" I muttered as I pulled on my white uniform. "Then I could have stayed home where it's warm."

I grabbed a bite to eat and headed for the car. A shocking blast of bitterly cold air hit me as soon as I opened the door. It may not have been a blizzard, but the wind was whipping past my face so fast that it took my breath away and stung my eyes. The snow that was already on the ground was drifting and the few flakes that were coming down were clinging to the drifting snow.

It was a terrible day to have to drive all the way to Ann Arbor, but I was used to snow and wind. I had grown up with it and had learned to drive in it. Besides, it was only a fifteen mile trip. Not that far. This was the way winter in the north was. So I let my dad's van warm up for a few minutes and slowly backed out of the driveway.

Things were quiet at school. Usually the salon was filled with women chatting away as they had their hair shampooed, cut, colored, and every other imaginable thing you can do to hair. But today it was quiet. Apparently not many women wanted to brave the wind and snow to have their hair styled. And even some of the girls had chosen not to come to school.

The radio was playing quietly in the background as the girls styled the hair of the few women who had come out. Suddenly one of the teachers called for everyone to be quiet.

"Listen to this," the teacher said.

The radio announcer had broken in on the music to give a winter storm warning. The blizzard that had been predicted for the night before had moved more slowly than anticipated, but it was picking up speed and headed our way. People in the Ann Arbor area were warned to avoid travel and to stay at home if possible. Businesses were told to close.

Now that was unusual. It takes some pretty bad weather to send people seeking shelter in Michigan. Even in the dead of winter. But one look out the window verified what the reporter was saying. The wind had already been strong, but now the snow was coming down in thick flakes and appeared to be getting thicker and thicker. It was swirling and whipping past so fast that you could barely see more than a few feet out the window.

The teacher told us all to go home. The school was closing for the day. Everyone hustled to get their coats on and gather their belongings. My classmates headed out to their cars and began to disappear out of the parking lot one by one.

I left with everyone else, but to my dismay, I could not coax the van to drive up the steep incline that lead onto the road in front of the school. I'd get part way up and the tires would just start spinning. So I backed down and tried again. No good. It still wouldn't make it up and out of the lot. What was I going to do?

I went back into the school and called my father. This was long before cell phones so I used a land line. Dad told me to stay put and he would come to get me. As the minutes ticked by, I could see this was truly developing into a blizzard. I had seen bad snow storms before, but this looked worse than anything I had ever seen. Certainly worse than anything I had ever driven in before!

The trip from our home town would have taken Dad about 15 minutes on a normal day, but today wasn't normal. I waited patiently, praying that Dad would be able to get through. Finally, after about 45 minutes I saw Dad's car pulling into the lot. He drove behind the van, jumped out of the car, and opened his trunk.

"What are you doing?" I shouted to Dad as I watched him lift a cement block from the car's trunk. He loaded it into the back of the van. I could barely hear his reply as he shouted back, "I'm weighing down the van. This will give it more traction. It's too light right now."

After he had loaded several blocks into the van, he slammed the trunk shut and indicated that I should drive the car. "Follow me," Dad shouted over the blowing wind and snow.

Amazingly, the van made it up the steep incline and onto the road. We began the slow trip home. We crept along, just inching our way along.

I didn't think it was possible, but it started to snow even harder. Now I couldn't see the road at all. I couldn't see the side of the road or the center line. I couldn't see more than a few feet in front of me. In fact, I couldn't even see the bright aqua body of the van ahead of me. The only thing I could see were Dad's red tail lights. Everything else looked like a solid wall of white wind.

I remember clutching the steering wheel tighter than I ever had before and I concentrated on following those tail lights. I was determined that I wouldn't let them get out of my sight. I knew if I did, I would be completely lost without a clue as to where the road was or where I was going.

I wouldn't let myself even think about the fact that I had no idea how dad was figuring out where the road was, or what would happen if I lost sight of those tail lights. I just stared ahead and began to pray.

It was strange, because normally I would be terrified in such a frightening situation. I'm a pretty big chicken when it comes to being brave about scary things, but I really wasn't that afraid that day. When I thought about it later I realized why. I knew that up ahead of me was my father. I knew he had driven this road since he was a boy. He knew the way. If I slid off the road or lost sight of his tail lights, Dad would come back for me. Dad wouldn't let anything happen to me. Even surrounded by the howling wind and blinding snow storm, I felt safe.

OUR PLACE OF PEACE

We can sometimes become lost in our storms. We can't see through our problems to what lies ahead. We don't know what to do and we don't know which way to go. All we can see is the terrible storm and it looks like there is no end in sight. In our desperate attempt to see the unknown, we lose our sense of peace.

But if we keep our eyes on our Heavenly Father, then we will be safe. We will have peace. God knows the path ahead of us. He is the One who planned it. He wants to be the One who leads us along it each day.

When the storms of life come up, God will not always make them go away, but He will safely lead us. If we stay close and keep our eyes on Him, we know we can go anywhere with our Father as our guide and protector.

That takes trust. But the most trustworthy One I know has proven He can be trusted. He has never let me down. Just as I knew my dad wouldn't let any harm come to me, it is also true that my Heavenly Father will also be my safe haven. Through every storm, He has proven to me that I can trust Him. That gives me peace.

It is the same for you. You can trust your Heavenly Father. He won't take away all the storms, but He will be there ahead of you to guide you safely to the place where you need to be in your life. He will be there to shelter you from the storm. Hide yourself in the rock of ages for He is your peace.

Calming Your Storm

- Identify your internal disrupters. Know the enemy. Often our internal disrupters are worse than any external disrupter could ever be. What disrupts you from within? God doesn't want you to have your peace disrupted by fear, anger, bitterness, guilt, or anything else. I may not have even touched on the thing that disrupts your peace. Ask God to show you if you don't already know. Then ask Him to help you eliminate it if that is His will.
- Identify your external disrupters. What disrupts you from without? Do people or circumstances rob you of peace? Ask God to show you how to handle your peace disrupters. Ask Him how you can deal with the situations or people in such a way that your peace would be restored while at the same time bringing glory to Him. You may need to live with it. Ask God to use it for His purpose even if you can't see the purpose in it.
- Try to view your storm from God's point of view. Ask Him to show you if what appears to be a terrible storm to you is really an allowed event that will order your steps and help you to become more Christ-like.

- Draw close to God. During the storms of life, you need all the help you can get. Don't turn away from the One who can give you peace. Turn to Him. Draw close to the heart of God. Don't spend time reading the Bible and praying because that is what you are required to do. Do it because you love God and you long to be close to Him. If you don't feel a longing to be close to Him, then develop that longing. Ask God to restore your desire to be close to Him. Consider your time with Him a privilege not a chore. Make it personal.
- Dwell on verses that talk about peace. There are hundreds of them. Think about what God is saying about how to have peace with Him and with others. Then put those verses into practice in your life.
- There are great hymns about peace. Sing them. "Hiding In Thee," "It Is Well," "Be Still, My Soul," "Day By Day," and many others.

MEMORIZE THESE VERSES

Isaiah 26:3 *Thou wilt keep him in perfect peace, whose mind is stayed on thee: because he trusteth in thee.*

John 14:27 *Peace I leave with you, my peace I give unto you: not as the world giveth, give I unto you. Let not your heart be troubled, neither let it be afraid.*

John 16:33 *These things I have spoken unto you, that in me ye might have peace. In the world ye shall have tribulation: but be of good cheer; I have overcome the world.*

Isaiah 32:17 *And the work of righteousness shall be peace; and the effect of righteousness quietness and assurance for ever.*

Joy in the Storm

MY JOY

I have to tell you this at the very beginning of this chapter. I really shouldn't. When I took composition in English class, and again when I studied about preparing a speech, all the teachers said you should always hold your strongest and most important point for last. That's for impact. But I can't wait that long. Besides, if I wait that long, you might mistake my strongest point on joy as being the most unimportant. So here goes.

God is my joy.

That simple statement is the most important thing I learned about joy during my journey through grief. It was something that took me awhile to comprehend and understand, but when I did grasp it fully, it changed my life.

God is my joy.

How can I explain that amazing fact to you so that you will understand? When I first found out about Bo's cancer, I thought I lost my joy. Everywhere I looked there was only sadness. Mom was sick. Bo was sick. We were all in financial debt. We were surrounded by grief and the future seemed awfully bleak.

I was certain I had lost my joy. I didn't feel any joy. It was all gone. I wasn't happy. I didn't feel like smiling very often. All I felt was pain. I can't tell you how often I crawled into bed at night, cradled in Gary's arms, and cried myself to sleep.

My joy just wasn't there. No matter where I looked, there was no cause to be joyful. My life seemed consumed with sadness. I ached emotionally and I felt like I would never experience joy again.

But then something happened. Joy began to seep back into my life and it dawned on me that my circumstance had not gotten any better. Everything was the same so that couldn't be the reason I was beginning to experience joy again. I realized that when I talked to God and when I spent time in His Word, I was gaining joy just by being with God. Joy was returning through His presence.

No, joy didn't just drop out of the sky and hit me on the head, but I slowly began to realize that just having a God I could turn to was joy. I realized that having a God who was in control was joy. Having a God who could do something while I was so helpless was joy. Do you understand?

It began to dawn on me. I wasn't going to find joy in the actual storm itself, but I could find joy in my God.

God is my joy.

I'm not saying God gives me joy. I'm not saying God allows me to experience joy in spite of my storm. While those statements are true, it goes deeper than that. I am saying that even in the storm, when no joy was to be found in any of my circumstances or in any of the people around me, and certainly not in my emotions, I found joy in God Himself.

Just knowing there was a Supreme Being who wouldn't have to give me a second thought, let alone love, guide, and protect me, but did - that was joy. The Creator of the Universe thinks about me. He understands me, loves me, guides and protects me. What joy!

Just knowing I had a God who loved me unconditionally and who had a purpose for my life was a joy. Just having someone who completely understood what I was feeling was a joy. Just having someone who could do what no other human on this earth could do was a joy. Knowing that I am God's and God is mine was joy.

When I fretted that I could do so little of true value for my kids, God could do exactly what they needed. When I had no money to give them help pay their bills, God had the riches of Heaven. When I stood by helplessly and watched my kids suffer, God did not have His hands tied. He was there beside them to give them strength. That knowledge brought joy to my heart.

I began tapping into the idea that God Himself is my source of joy. My joy is not just a feeling, my joy is a person. My joy isn't something passing that is influenced by circumstances. My joy is not some flimsy thing that comes and goes according to what is happening at the time. My joy is a person who is eternal and unchanging. My joy is solid, permanent, and everlasting, because my joy is God.

God is my joy!

If you can grasp onto that fact, then it can help you to experience joy also. You don't have to go looking for some ecstatic feeling. You don't have to try to work up some happy facts about your sad situation. Instead, you can rest in the certainty that though you may not FEEL joy for a period of time, you can know that you have not lost your joy because you cannot lose your God. Your joy does not have to depend on a feeling, it can be rock solid in a person. And not just any person. Your joy can be your God.

I think that is what God meant when He was talking to Abraham in Genesis 15. Abraham was feeling sad and troubled because even though God had given him great wealth and power, he had no son to pass it on to. That was important to him. So Abraham was feeling pretty low. God spoke to Abraham. He told Abraham that He Himself was his exceeding great reward. Not riches or land. Not a son to pass his riches to. Not anything that people think of as bringing happiness and joy. God Himself was Abraham's great reward.

Genesis 15:1 says, *After these things the word of the LORD came unto Abram in a vision, saying, Fear not, Abram: I am thy shield, and thy exceeding great reward.*

God was saying, "I am your reward. Your reward is not some mere thing that comes and goes. It's ME that is your reward. And you always have Me."

When God told Moses to tell Pharaoh to release the Israelites, Moses balked. He thought no one would believe Him. God told Moses to tell everyone that "I AM" had sent him. "I AM" is the name of God.

When God told Moses, "I AM," we can't even begin to take in the scope of what God was telling him. He was telling Moses that He is everything that he could ever need and more. He was saying, "I AM the great Creator and Sustainer. I AM the great keeper of all wisdom. I AM always present and aware. I AM in complete control. I AM all you will ever need for time and eternity." He was saying "When you need strength, I AM your strength. When you need power, I AM your power. When you need courage, I AM your courage. I AM everything."

The same is true for joy. God, the great I AM, is your joy. When you are surrounded by grief and sadness in life, turn to the great I AM. He will say to you, "I AM your joy."

David knew God was his joy. In Psalm 43:4 David specifically refers to God as being his exceeding joy. David didn't say, God gives me exceeding joy." He said, "God is my exceeding joy." He must have understood that important fact.

Then will I go unto the altar of God, unto God my exceeding joy: yea, upon the harp will I praise thee, O God my God.

When I thought my joy was gone, God said to my heart, "I AM your joy. Joy is not some mere feeling that only comes when things are going your way. I AM your joy even when the worst storm you could ever experience is sweeping over you. Look at ME. I AM your joy!"

I hope you can grasp that. I always feel at a loss to explain what I mean. Words are never enough. It's just something that came to my heart and completely changed the way I faced my storm. It didn't make everything all better. It didn't mean I no longer had pain and sorrow. It meant that even in my pain and grief, I knew my joy was still intact because my God was intact. I hadn't lost a thing. I hadn't lost my joy because I hadn't lost my God.

IN THE DEPTHS

Before I go any further, let me tell you that there were days when I didn't want to feel joy. I was so broken that joy and happiness were feelings that did not appeal to me. I won't say I enjoyed my misery. I didn't. But I just didn't have any room for joy.

There were times when joy seemed like a betrayal to the ones I loved so much. How could I even think of laughing or being happy when Bo and Rynda were experiencing such pain? How could I have joy when Bo was gone and would never return?

You may feel that way sometimes. You feel guilty to experience anything less than the pain that seems to have taken over your life. You just want to shut out all joy and comfort. You don't want it.

There are those times. There are times when you don't want to try to conjure up joy. And during those times, I think it is okay to hurt and cry. It's okay to grieve. In fact, it's important.

If you are at that point in your storm where joy is not something you can face, then just rest in the fact that you don't need to have a feeling of joy to be in possession of the God who is your joy. Like I said before, you don't have to conjure up a feeling, just know that you have a God who is your joy. You can never lose Him. He is always close beside you.

REASONS FOR JOY

I won't tell you that I ever got to the point where I enjoyed my storm. It never ceased to be painful and difficult. But I did find reasons to have joy in spite of the storm. God was my joy, but there were also times when God so mercifully gave me a feeling of joy within the storm.

I think there are reasons to experience joy in the storm. Some reasons for joy can be for our benefit and some can be as a testimony that benefits others. Either way, having joy in the storm can have a tremendous impact on everyone. Here are some reasons I found for joy in my storm.

I Have Salvation And A Savior.

Not everyone knows that they are saved from their sins and on their way to an eternity in Heaven. They hope so. They work hard to earn salvation. But they don't know for sure. You and I, if we have accepted Christ as our personal Savior, know for sure. We have the joy of our Salvation.

In the following passage the prophet Habakkuk writes about a storm God showed him what was awaiting Israel. He speaks of the fear and unrest the impending storm caused within him. But then he says, "Even with all the terrible things that will come against us, I am determined to have joy because my joy is in my God who gives salvation."

Habakkuk 3:16-18 says, *When I heard, my belly trembled; my lips quivered at the voice: rottenness entered into my bones, and I trembled in myself, that I might rest in the day of trouble: when he cometh up unto the people, he will invade them with his troops.*

Although the fig tree shall not blossom, neither shall fruit be in the vines; the labour of the olive shall fail, and the fields shall yield no meat; the flock shall be cut off from the fold, and there shall be no herd in the stalls.

Yet I will rejoice in the LORD, I will joy in the God of my salvation.

Our greatest blessing in all of life is our salvation. It is more than we deserve. It is more than anything we could ever hope to achieve on our own. I heard a saying once and I think it is an interesting thing to ponder. It goes, "If God never did a single thing for you beyond giving you salvation, would you still love and praise Him?"

The answer should be "Yes, my salvation is more than I deserve." But I know that I certainly have a long "wish list" that I pray about all the time. I constantly go to God asking for more. Don't we all? Sure. We have all sorts of things that we think we want from God in order to be happy. But take the time to realize that God could have given you salvation and then retreated to Heaven until the time when you die. That could have been all He ever did for you and it would have been more than enough.

Even if God gave you nothing beyond salvation, you could still find such joy in that wonderful gift. But He didn't just give you salvation and stop there. God gives so much more. He gives you a Savior whose mere presence brings joy.

Isaiah 61:10 says, *I will greatly rejoice in the LORD, my soul shall be joyful in my God; for he hath clothed me with the garments of salvation, he hath covered me with the robe of righteousness, as a bridegroom decketh himself with ornaments, and as a bride adorneth herself with her jewels.*

God does not stop at salvation in His generosity toward you. Not only do you have salvation, you also have a Savior. Jesus Christ promises He will never leave nor forsake you. He promises to guide you each step of the way. He protects and provides. He sits in Heaven, constantly interceding for you.

In the stormy times of life it may seem that somehow God has dropped the ball. "After all, if God protects, then why did I have an accident or get cancer? If God provides, then why don't I have all the money I need? If God is always with me, then why didn't He prevent this bad thing from happening to me?"

I don't know, but I just have to trust. What I do know is that no matter what problems I must face in life, I know I have a Savior, Jesus Christ, who promises to always be by my side. It is a joy to know I do not face my storms alone. The One who loved me enough to leave Heaven and come to earth to die a terrible death so my sins could be forgiven is the same One who will always be with me. That is joy.

I Have Two-Way Contact With God.

I have a Sunday Bible that I keep with my sermon notebook and purse. I have a Bible that I received for Christmas when I was quite young and it's a mess, but I'd never part with it. I have a small white Bible that I carried when I was a junior Maid of Honor in my brother's wedding. I have about five study Bibles that I use when I am writing my Children's Church materials and Vacation Bible School programs. My husband has more Bibles than I do. You probably have lots of Bibles in your home too.

It hasn't been that long, in the big scheme of things, since Bibles were not so common-place. Not so many centuries ago people couldn't afford a Bible and even if they could, they might not have had the education to read it. Further back in history, the Bible wasn't even completely written. Many Old Testament people only had the few books that Moses had written. Before Moses, they only had the spoken Word of God. Before there was a Bible at all, God came to personally speak to men.

God has always made Himself known to men. You and I are so fortunate to be able to take God's precious Word in our hands at any time we choose. We can know what God wants us to know. We can draw comfort and peace and joy from what God tells us.

David found great joy in God's Word. Read the entire 119th Psalm.

Psalm 119:162 says, *I rejoice at thy word, as one that findeth great spoil.*

Jeremiah 15:16 says, *Thy words were found, and I did eat them; and thy word was unto me the joy and rejoicing of mine heart: for I am called by thy name, O LORD God of hosts.*

Scripture tells us that Jesus often quoted the Old Testament during His time on earth. He depended on God's Word. He also took time to communicate directly with His Father. Often he would go alone to pray. You can do the same. You can know and use God's Word and you can go alone and talk with the One who can truly help during your time of storm.

What a joy to know that God wants to have personal contact with you. He speaks through His Word and He listens when you pray. Everything you need to help you survive your storm is contained in God's Word and God's presence.

You can go to God at any time and He is ready, willing, and eager to listen. Even when you feel like your prayers haven't gotten farther than the ceiling, you can know for a fact that God is listening. It may not seem that way to you, but God's Word says He is listening.

Psalm 116:2 says, *Because he hath inclined his ear unto me, therefore will I call upon him as long as I live.*

Hebrews 4:16 says, *Let us therefore come boldly unto the throne of grace, that we may obtain mercy, and find grace to help in time of need.*

Spend time with the Word so you can have your needs met. If you are having trust issues, find out what God has to say about trust. The same is true for peace, joy, safety, and comfort. It is through God's Word and prayer that you find value and purpose in your storms. Go to Him often. Joy in the fact that you can open and study God's Word. Joy in the fact that you can talk to your loving Father, the King of kings.

His Ways Are Best.

In the midst of a storm, nothing seems to make sense. Everything seems confusing. Our eyes are blinded and our hearts are sick. We often don't understand why God has allowed such a thing to happen. What good could come from this situation?

I understand that. I certainly would not choose a storm. But joy comes from knowing that God always does what is best. God's ways are always best. Faith demands that you and I turn to God and trust Him to do what is good and right.

When your world has been turned upside-down, you have to trust that God is not upside-down also. You have to trust that He is bigger than your small universe. You have to trust that He is still in control.

You may never know here on earth why something happened, but you can know that God not only knows, He has a purpose. If you have faith that God has a purpose, then you can have the joy of knowing His purpose will be fulfilled. Whatever God is doing, He is doing it for your good and for His glory. Nothing can stop God from achieving His goals.

Isaiah 55:6-12 says, *Seek ye the LORD while he may be found, call ye upon him while he is near:*

Let the wicked forsake his way, and the unrighteous man his thoughts: and let him return unto the LORD, and he will have mercy upon him; and to our God, for he will abundantly pardon.

For my thoughts are not your thoughts, neither are your ways my ways, saith the LORD.

For as the heavens are higher than the earth, so are my ways higher than your ways, and my thoughts than your thoughts.

For as the rain cometh down, and the snow from heaven, and returneth not thither, but watereth the earth, and maketh it bring forth and bud, that it may give seed to the sower, and bread to the eater:

So shall my word be that goeth forth out of my mouth: it shall not return unto me void, but it shall accomplish that which I please, and it shall prosper in the thing whereto I sent it.

For ye shall go out with joy, and be led forth with peace: the mountains and the hills shall break forth before you into singing, and all the trees of the field shall clap their hands.

You and I can't understand God's ways. They are far beyond our small capacity of reasoning. But God assures us He knows what He is doing. He assures us His ways will lead to joy.

I Can Bring Glory To God.

You are not alone in this world. There are those around you who are watching, especially when you are in a storm. Others know you are having problems. They are watching to see how you handle your problems.

Christians watch. If they can see joy in your life, despite your trials and griefs, then they will be encouraged and helped with the trials they are facing. There were many times I heard people say that when they went to the hospital to encourage Bo, by the end of the visit Bo had encouraged them because of the joy he displayed in his life.

People who need the Lord are watching. They wonder if your God is real. They have heard the things you tell them, now they are watching to see if you really live what you have said. They also wonder if your God can be of any help to them. They have no one to face the storm with them. They are alone. They are lost and helpless. They may not feel that way when things are going well for them, but there will come a day when they must face life's storms. The way you react to your storm today can help them know who to turn to in their storm tomorrow.

If you can find joy in your storm, then your life can be a testimony to God. Your life can bring glory to Him. Others will see what a great God you love and serve.

I Peter 1:6-8 says, *Wherein ye greatly rejoice, though now for a season, if need be, ye are in heaviness through manifold temptations:*

That the trial of your faith, being much more precious than of gold that perisheth, though it be tried with fire, might be found unto praise and honour and glory at the appearing of Jesus Christ:

Whom having not seen, ye love; in whom, though now ye see him not, yet believing, ye rejoice with joy unspeakable and full of glory.

I Peter 4:12-13 says, *Beloved, think it not strange concerning the fiery trial which is to try you, as though some strange thing happened unto you:*

But rejoice, inasmuch as ye are partakers of Christ's sufferings; that, when his glory shall be revealed, ye may be glad also with exceeding joy.

You may not be experiencing much "laugh out loud" kind of joy right now, but if you allow God to be your joy and allow Him to shine through your life, then future and eternal joy will be yours. What a joy it is to bring glory to God through your life!

Expressions Of Joy

Thankfulness and gratitude are true expressions of joy. But oh, how hard it is to be thankful during the hard times. There are days when it is hard to find something to be thankful for. But you can be thankful you have a God. If God is your joy, then you have great cause to rejoice.

Psalm 31:7 says, *I will be glad and rejoice in thy mercy: for thou hast considered my trouble; thou hast known my soul in adversities.*

The day after Bo was hospitalized for the first time, Bo and Rynda decided to start a "Blessings Book." It wasn't anything fancy, just a regular notebook, but it would hold words that caused joy and true expressions of thankfulness. It was a simple thing that became a fountainhead of great joy.

Every time something good happened, Bo and Rynda would write it down so they could remember what God was doing for them. Every time someone helped them, in the book it would be recorded. Every time God answered a prayer, it would be written in the book. Every time someone called to offer a word of encouragement, it was noted.

Bo and Rynda knew times would be hard from then on. There would be days they would get discouraged. There would be days nothing would seem to go right. There would be days when they would wonder if God even remembered about them.

On those days, they would pull out the "Blessings Book." They would read how God had blessed them, provided for them, and answered their prayers.

That book became an important source of strength and joy for them. It reminded them that they had a God who loved them and cared for them, even in the hard times.

Also, at the very beginning of Bo's hospital stays, he and Rynda decided they would make an effort to say thank you to everyone who did anything for them in the hospital. Often patients in hospitals complain about the bland food, about how slowly the nurses respond, about having to give blood every few hours. Bo and Rynda decided not to be complainers.

Instead, when the housekeeper mopped the floor, they said, "Thank you." When the guy from food services brought the food tray, even if Bo couldn't eat, they said, "Thank you." When the nurses' aides came to change the bedding, they would say, "Thank you." When the nurse came to draw blood or give Bo medicine, they would say, "Thank you." When the technicians did bone marrow biopsies, they said, "Thank you."

Nothing was too small or insignificant for a word of thanks. And soon, Bo was a favorite on the cancer floor. Everyone knew Bo and his smiling face, kind words, and thankful spirit. Even when he felt terrible, Bo radiated the joy of the Lord.

Over the next four years, as they went in and out of the hospital, they kept their Blessings Book. Over the next four years, they said, "Thank you." Over the next four years, they made an impact on everyone they met as having a sweet testimony for God.

Psalm 103:2 says, *Bless the LORD, O my soul, and forget not all his benefits.*

Even when you can't see any joy in your storm, you can still pull joy from having a grateful and thankful spirit. When you give thanks to God and to those around you, you will be amazed at the joy you experience. You can't be thankful without having joy flow back to you.

LOOKING FOR JOY

Find joy where you can. Search for it. Savor it. Then pass it on.

There is joy to be found in the storm because God is there in the storm. You do not go through your storm by yourself. God is with you and that alone is joy. But you will find that God sends you joy in some of the least expected places.

I love cats. Kittens are adorable, but I even love cats when they are old and set in their ways.

When I was a young girl, we lived in the country. We didn't live on a farm, like my grandparents, but we did live several miles out of town.

The Eye of the Storm

Our home was bordered on two sides by farmers' fields that contained things like wheat, corn, and soybeans.

My mother was never very fond of animals, but since we lived where we could have animals outside without too much trouble, she allowed me to have them. We usually had one dog. We always had at least three cats. At times there were more.

I loved my cats. When I was still young enough to play with dolls, I would often enlist one of my cats to fill the role of being my baby. Several of my cats wouldn't cooperate with me at all, but I had one dear cat that actually seemed to enjoy the game. Poor kitty would be dressed up in my doll's clothes and swaddled in blankets. I would carry it around and play house.

Stray cats often wandered through our backyard. I suppose they were just passing through, but I wanted to make sure they would stay, so I would rush into the house, find a plastic tub of some sort, and fill it with milk. Then out I would run to feed the cat and give it plenty of attention. By the time I was finished lavishing love, attention, and food on them, nearly every cat I encountered decided they had found a new home.

My mom would look out the window a few days later and comment to my dad, "We seem to have a new cat hanging around. Why on earth do all the stray cats in the state seem to find their way to our house?" I'd just smile a knowing smile and keep silent while I went to get another bowl of milk.

When Gary and I got married my cat days were over. We lived in a trailer and traveled full-time. We rarely stayed in a state for more than five days. I never even tried to put a cat in the truck or trailer and drag it from state to state each week. I knew that while I enjoyed the traveling, a cat probably wouldn't.

Another reason I knew we couldn't have a cat was because we had a rabbit that lived with us. We used the rabbit for our Gospel magic tricks. I'll admit, rabbits are nice. They can be very loving and I was amazed at how smart they are. We had several over the many years we were on the road. But I missed my cats tremendously. I often wished I could have a cat, but it was not to be.

A very short time after we discovered Bo had cancer the Lord sent me a kitten. I have always felt strongly that the kitten was sent to bring joy into my life just at the time I needed it most.

Joy in the Storm

One day Gary and I walked from our office building that is located behind my parents' house onto their back porch. Out catapulted a little ball of black, white, and caramel colored fur. It was the cutest little calico kitten I had ever seen. The poor thing had been hiding under the barbecue grill cover. She ran up to me and began frantically crying her heart out. When I knelt down to talk to her, she jumped into my arms.

It didn't take long to discover why she had been hiding. The other cats on the property did not like her one little bit. They hissed at her and tried to chase her away. So she hid until she found a human with which to plead her case.

She obviously had been dropped off by someone who no longer wanted her. She was very lost and very hungry. She desperately needed a friend. And she had been smart enough to jump into the exact pair of arms of the one who would never want to let her go.

I held her tight and rubbed her head. She began to purr. That was it for me. My heart melted. I was sold. I considered running for a saucer of milk, but I could tell the kitten had already decided she was home. I was in total agreement, but Gary wasn't sold yet. He admitted that she was cute, but he mentioned how expensive shots and spaying could be. Besides, Mom and Dad already had two other cats on the property.

I went to work finding a local animal group that offered everything she needed for a much lower price than the vet charged, so Gary agreed to let me keep her. I named her Zoe.

After all these years, I finally have a cat of my own. And Zoe knows she is mine. She always comes to me first and will completely ignore everyone else if I am within sight. She cuddles on my lap. She talks to me. When I enter a room she'll get up and come greet me. She sits smack dab in the middle of my keyboard when I'm trying to work and she demands to be petted. She loves to play and she is so funny to watch. She's wonderful!

What joy she brings to me. And she came at a time when I needed her most! Even when I was deep in sorrow, Zoe could always bring a smile to my face as I watched her crazy antics or just held her. It may sound silly, but I believe God can bring us joy, even in little ways. I feel that Zoe is one of God's little extra joys that He gave to me in the midst of my storm. Whenever I look at her, even now, I think of God's gift of joy to me.

So, find joy in the little things around you. Maybe it will be in the laughter of your child, or the kindness that someone shows to you, or in a beautiful sunset. God sends joy in some unlikely ways. Be on the alert and allow that joy to be a source of strength and encouragement to you.

Count Your Blessings

When I was a young teen, I determined in my heart that I would serve the Lord with my life. I didn't exactly know what God had in mind for me, but I thought He might want me to marry a missionary. I wasn't too far from wrong. As you know, the man the Lord brought into my life was an evangelist.

We loved life on the road. Every week there were new places to see and new people to meet. In the late afternoons, before evening service, we would go to people's homes for dinner. We met people from every state and ate in homes almost every night of the year. We met some very interesting people and saw some very interesting places.

One evening we went to eat with a lady who had quietly approached us and asked if we would like to come to her house. We said, "Yes," and the next evening we parked our truck in front of her house and went inside.

The lady had explained the night before that she lived alone with her daughter. Her husband had died many years before. The two women lived in a small home with modest furnishings. The woman's daughter was forty-two years old, but she was not like a normal forty-two year old person. This woman's daughter was severely retarded. She had the mental capacity of a very young child and was totally unable to communicate or care for herself.

The dear lady answered the door and invited us to come in. She asked us to sit in the living room while she finished dinner. A quick look around the room showed that it was very sparsely decorated. Nothing fancy. But it was neat and clean.

In one corner sat an organ. Gary loves organ music, so when the lady re-entered the living room, Gary asked if she played. She replied that she did.

"Would you play a song for us?" Gary asked.

"Oh, yes," she replied with a smile on her face. "I'll play my favorite song."

The lady sat down and soon the room was filled with the beautiful sounds of her favorite song. It was "Count Your Blessings."

As I sat and listened to the song, a lump caught in my throat. I swiped at my eyes to wipe away the tears that were running down my face.

"This is amazing," I thought. "Here is this dear lady. I was feeling sorry for her. She has no husband. She doesn't have much money. She has a daughter who needs constant care who will never grow up. She has so many problems! Yet here she sits, playing 'Count Your Blessings.' She could have been counting all the worries in her life. Or counting all the bitter, angry feelings that most people in her situation would be experiencing. But instead, she was counting her blessings!"

What a wonderful testimony to her Lord. Here was a woman who instead of complaining about how unfair life had been to her, was instead praising God for all the good things He had done for her.

I am sure, that many years before, this lady discovered that even though life was not always fair, if she thanked God for His blessings, then He would be pleased with her. He would see her thankful heart.

This lady didn't have much, but she counted the blessings she did have. She didn't look at the bad, she looked at the good. And certainly God HAD given her many blessings. She had found that happiness came from a thankful heart, not a bitter heart.

Often God gives us blessings but we fail to be thankful. Instead, we focus our attention on the things we think are bad and unfair. We think of all we wish we had. We stew and fret and complain. Our hearts are heavy and we lose our song in life. We don't see that God has allowed what we think are bad things into our life for a reason and a purpose. We don't see that life on earth is never perfect, but God still daily loads us with so many blessings.

You can have joy in your storm, but it is not something that is always expressed by walking around laughing and acting like nothing difficult is happening in your life. It's the quiet joy of knowing you have a God who is your personal, ever-present, and all-powerful Father. Life's storms are not easy. They are not joyful. But joy is found in God. Cling to Him and search His face for the smile of His blessings and you will find joy.

Let God be your joy.

Calming Your Storm

Life seems useless without joy. But fortunately for us, God is the source of joy. And God delights in giving us joy.

- If you feel you have lost your joy, don't despair. Give yourself time. Know that the God, who is the source of joy, will give you joy. Look to God to be your joy.

• Look up verses on joy, gladness, happiness, and blessedness. These are all words that God uses to refer to joy. See what God has to say about joy. Spend time thinking about the verses you look up. Let them become a part of your life.

• Spend some "one-on-one" time with God. Ask Him to restore your joy. Ask Him to bring back your joy. Ask Him to show you that He is your joy.

• Find ways to express your joy. Be grateful for God's blessings. Say, "Thank you," to God and to those who surround you. Maybe there is someone who has done some service for you that seems small and insignificant. Remember to thank them. You will be surprised at how a "Thank you" can bring joy to others while at the same time bringing joy to you also.

• Count your blessings. If you haven't already started a Blessings Book, do it now. As you begin to count your blessings, you will find that just seeing how God has blessed is a joy. Reread the book often to remind yourself of past blessings.

• Look for joy in the little things in life. You may be surprised at the things that provide joy. When you find small joys, record them in your Blessings Book. Then thank God for them.

• Sing songs of joy. There are many songs such as "Count Your Blessings," "Come, Thou Fount," "For the Beauty of the Earth," "Great is Thy Faithfulness," "I Will Sing the Wondrous Story," "O For A Thousand Tongues," "What A Friend We Have in Jesus," and many more.

MEMORIZE THESE VERSES

John 16:22 *And ye now therefore have sorrow: but I will see you again, and your heart shall rejoice, and your joy no man taketh from you.*

Psalm 31:7 says, *I will be glad and rejoice in thy mercy: for thou hast considered my trouble; thou hast known my soul in adversities.*

Psalm 51:12 *Restore unto me the joy of thy salvation; and uphold me with thy free spirit.*

Psalm 16:11 *Thou wilt shew me the path of life: in thy presence is fulness of joy.*

Safe in the Storm

Our Anchor

As a teenager I loved spending my summers at our cottage on Wampler's Lake in Michigan. One thing I enjoyed was the fact that each summer when we moved up there, I went from being an only child to having a little brother. Okay, Brad wasn't my little brother, but he seemed like one. My cousin, Brad, is just two years younger than I am. He also spent the summers at the lake at his cottage which was next door to ours.

I'm not an only child, but I always think of myself that way. I have no sisters. I have one brother, Jerry, and he is fifteen years older than I am. When I was three years old, Jerry joined the Navy. Shortly before Jerry got out of the Navy, he got married. So I don't remember my brother ever living at home and he always seemed more like an uncle when I was young.

Brad was like my little brother and we were inseparable during the summer months. We got along great. Sure, sometimes we would argue about little things. I remember one day he got angry at me and shouted, "Everything you want is peaches and cream, but everything I want is . . . is. . . is moldy raisins and bread!" It's been one of my favorite sayings ever since. But most of the time we got along famously.

Behind our cottage was a small trailer that my dad had built years before. Dad never towed it anywhere anymore. It just sat behind the cottage and served as an extra room. Brad and I took it over as a game room. We set up our record player and cassette player. We combined all our tapes and records. On the table we would set up a Monopoly board. The game would start at the beginning of the summer and it often lasted until the summer's end. We would only play in snatches during quiet evenings or on rainy days when the weather was no good for swimming.

Since you can't play Monopoly or even swim all summer long, we also devised other things to occupy our time. Most days we would walk up to the historic shrine on U.S. 12 and walk through it. We rode our bikes. We played Hide-and-Seek and Kick-the-Can with the neighbor kids.

We also turned TPing the neighbors' homes into an art form. We would purchase as many boxes of Kleenex as we could afford or talk our moms into buying. Then we would sit in the trailer and make tissue flowers for hours on end. When we had several bags of roses and other colorful flowers, we would sneak out after dark and decorate a friend's home and car. The next morning all our neighbors awoke to the sight of someone's lawn that looked more like a float from the Rose Bowl Parade than a yard. After everyone had "ooed" and "aahed," we would go offer to clean it up. After all, the goal was our entertainment, not making enemies.

Another fun thing Brad and I discovered was Joanne. I know Joanne was not a "thing," but she was fun. She was a lady who lived a few cottages away from us. She had no children and her husband was away all week at his job. He would only come to the lake on the weekends. So Joanne was lonely and she enjoyed young people. Or at least she put up with us.

Joanne had a nice big, shiny new pontoon boat that we loved. Brad's folks had a speedboat but we rarely got to use it. My folks had a beat up old row boat which we had no desire to use. Not cool at all!

We often took Joanne's pontoon out for rides on the lake. Joanne was always just along for the ride. Brad was the designated captain and I helped to cast off and tie up when we were leaving or returning to the dock. We loved to go boating with Joanne.

Joanne's pontoon was big, but it wasn't very powerful. It only putted along at a top speed of 5 m.p.h. That was normal for most pontoons, but we loved to tease the owners of some of the bigger, more powerful speedboats on the lake. There was one pontoon on our lake that had been converted into a ski boat that could pull three to four skiers. It had a car engine in it and it was powerful. That pontoon could really move! It could outrun most of the speedboats on the lake. So when we pulled alongside a sleek power boat and called out a challenge to race, they took us seriously.

Brad would shout out, "One, Two, Three!" and off raced the power boat at top speeds while we inched along at 5 m.p.h.. It was funny to see the expressions on the faces of the speedboat owners as they looked back and realized that we had no power whatsoever.

Most often we just cruised slowly along without tormenting other boaters. Some afternoons we would stop the boat in the middle of the lake and anchor it while we all swam.

One evening a bunch of us kids from the neighborhood decided we wanted to go swimming off of Joanne's pontoon. Joanne was excited because that past weekend her husband had bought a brand new anchor to put on the pontoon. It was a beauty. It was twice as big as the old anchor they had owned.

That was good because the old anchor had not been able to hold the pontoon in place. The anchor would sink to the bottom, but it just skirted along the sandy bottom, not catching on anything and not heavy enough to hold the boat in one place. Often when we anchored to swim, the pontoon would begin to drift with the wind and current. After a half hour or so, we were surprised to find ourselves in a totally different spot from the one where we had originally dropped anchor. That wouldn't happen anymore with this new anchor. It was sure to do the job.

Joanne's husband had already placed the anchor on the boat, so we jumped aboard and shoved off. That evening we were definitely going to go swimming in the middle of the lake. We wanted to be the first to drop the anchor over the side.

Out to the center of the lake we went. When we picked the perfect spot, the anchor was hoisted up and dropped into the lake. Down, down, down it went. The rope was playing out quickly. The lake was quite deep where we had stopped and we couldn't begin to see the bottom. Then, all of a sudden, the end of the rope whizzed past us and down into the water it went as it followed the anchor on down to the floor of the lake.

We couldn't believe it! Then Joanne remembered. She hadn't tied the anchor to the boat. Apparently her husband had warned her to tie it or not use it until he returned the following weekend. She forgot.

Several of the guys dived in after it, but it was no use. It was gone! We stared after it in dismay for the longest time as if looking into the depths of the lake would somehow cause that anchor to come back up to us. But it didn't.

Eventually it became a joke for all of us, but no one was laughing that night. The expensive new anchor was gone in a second's time and there was no hope of ever finding it at the bottom of the lake. It's still down there.

That fancy new anchor did us no good. Why? Wasn't it a good anchor? Sure. It was a great anchor, but it wasn't tied to the boat. It was useless without being secured to the boat. It did no good at all.

You and I are like boats on the sea of life. We have an anchor, but unless we are tied to the anchor that will keep us from drifting away or being carried about with the winds that blow around us, then our anchor cannot help us.

Jesus Christ is your anchor and Heaven is the harbor for which you sail. Like a ship in a fierce storm that is being tossed about, the only thing that can save you during the storms of life is to be fastened safe and secure to your anchor. You must hold fast to Christ. He is your safety. He is your only hope for standing fast until you reach the harbor.

How important it is to be secured, fast and sure, to your anchor, Jesus Christ. When you are held by Him, you can know that no currents can carry you off course, no winds can blow you away, no sudden wave can overturn you. If you are not tied to your anchor, you are without hope.

In times of storm you must cling to Him, but it is important to be tied safely to Him long before the storm comes. When the storm begins to rage all around, it may be too late to try to find a way to tie your anchor securely. It certainly won't be as easy as it would be when you are on calm seas. How much better if you are prepared before your ship ever casts off from the dock.

By staying close to Jesus Christ, by tying yourself to His love and care, you can be sure all is shipshape. You will be ready to weather any storm and know you will be safe.

Hebrews 6:17-20 says, *Wherein God, willing more abundantly to shew unto the heirs of promise the immutability of his counsel, confirmed it by an oath:*

That by two immutable things, in which it was impossible for God to lie, we might have a strong consolation, who have fled for refuge to lay hold upon the hope set before us:

Which hope we have as an anchor of the soul, both sure and stedfast, and which entereth into that within the veil;

Whither the forerunner is for us entered, even Jesus, made an high priest for ever after the order of Melchisedec.

Safe in the Storm

I love the song *We Have an Anchor* by Priscilla Owens,

> We have an anchor that keeps the soul
> Steadfast and sure while the billows roll.
> Fastened to the Rock which cannot move,
> Grounded firm and deep in the Savior's love.

OUR SHELTER

For you land lubbers, let's talk about safe shelter on solid ground. You don't have to be at sea to experience a storm.

When a storm hits, the first thing you do is seek shelter. Now, there are two types of storms. There is the kind of storm that gives you plenty of warning. You can watch it from a distance as the clouds move toward you. You have time to gather things you have left out in the yard and time to roll up the car windows. Time to find a place of shelter.

There is also the storm that just seems to come out of nowhere and burst on top of you. You look up in surprise as the winds whip and the rain comes down in torrents. There is no warning. No time to put away last minute things. No time to seek shelter in advance.

Life's storms can play out slowly, giving you plenty of time to think and try to prepare, giving you more time than you desire to suffer and grieve. Or they can burst upon you, taking you by complete surprise. Regardless of how much advance warning you receive, it is instinctive to seek shelter from a storm. It's just natural to look for a place where you can feel safe and where you will be protected.

But not all places of shelter are the same. Some are definitely more desirable than others.

Possibly you have looked in all the wrong places for a safe shelter. You have looked to others, to money, to technology, to your own wit and wisdom. But all you found was a flimsy excuse of a shelter. There was no true shelter in any of those places.

During the summers of my youth, we often swam while it was raining, but never if there was lightning. I've seen lightning hit the water during a storm. We didn't swim during high winds either. The waves, even on our small lake, could get quite rough. When the storms got rough, we left the lake and went seeking shelter.

The Eye of the Storm

My mother always told me never to hide under a tree as shelter during a lightning storm. That would be the worst place to go since lightning is more likely to hit a tree than anything else when you are out in a field.

I don't imagine a tent would be the most desirable place to be either. When Gary and I traveled we lived in an Airstream trailer, if we had a free week between meetings, we would often find a local state park where we could camp. Many times we would be parked alongside a campsite that was occupied by a family in a tent.

Sleeping on the ground and cooking by a campfire didn't greatly appeal to me, but it looked like it could be fun for a very limited amount of time. Yet when a storm would start to brew, I was never once tempted to leave the safety of my trailer and swap places with the people in the tent. It didn't look safe and I wondered if the people inside were dry and cozy like I was.

When I was fifteen years old, Mom, Dad, Aunt Ruth, Uncle Tom, cousin Nancy, and I took a monthlong trip to California. We took the southern route going out west and the northern route coming back east. We visited every major historic site and tourist trap worth seeing.

Behind the station wagon we towed a pop-up camper. Every night we would find a camp ground. Dad and Uncle Tom would get to work setting up the camper. Most of the upper parts of the camper were canvas and everything inside turned into a bed. There was room for all six of us to sleep. Not much room, but room.

One night it began to rain. As I lay in bed, I noticed the canvas was glistening as if it were covered with dew. In my ignorance I reached up and touched a spot on the canvas that was only a few inches above where my face was resting in the bed. For the rest of the night a slow but steady drip, drip, drip came down on my head and pillow. No one told me never to touch canvas when it was raining. How was I to know it would be like cutting a hole in the tent? I never touched it again.

Every morning the camper had to be packed up, even when the canvas was wet. When it was set up again in the evening, everything inside would be wet. It was miserable. The night before we left on our big trip out west, Nancy and I begged our folks to let us sleep in the camper. By the end of the trip we had no desire to ever see that camper again. I've never been tempted to go anywhere in a pop-up since then.

A tree, a tent, a camper. All of those shelters lack any real element of protection and security from a storm. They are weak and vulnerable. None of them would be my first choice for shelter.

No, I would much rather have something strong, sturdy, waterproof, and built on a firm foundation. The tent was better than a tree, the trailer was better than a tent, but a house is better than them all.

How can you find protection and safety from your storm? Easy, go to God. Spend time in prayer talking to Him. Spend time in His Word seeing what He has to say to you. Hide in Him. Let Him be your fortress of safety.

Psalm 27:5 says, *For in the time of trouble he shall hide me in his pavilion: in the secret of his tabernacle shall he hide me; he shall set me up upon a rock.*

In your Christian life, you will find that in times of danger, when you desperately need shelter, the stronger and more secure the shelter, the safer you will be. If you are wise, you will run to the only One who offers true protection in your storm. You will run to the Rock who is your firm foundation.

God is a mighty fortress. He is not a tent, not a trailer, not even a house. He is a rock solid fortress with an unshakable foundation. He is the only certain place of safety in which you can hide. No matter what storm may be brewing on your horizon or is possibly already beating down on your head, you can find refuge in God, your fortress.

Psalm 18:2 says, *The LORD is my rock, and my fortress, and my deliverer; my God, my strength, in whom I will trust; my buckler, and the horn of my salvation, and my high tower.*

Jeremiah 16:19 says, *O LORD, my strength, and my fortress, and my refuge in the day of affliction.*

In life you will experience many storms. Over and over you will need to run to your rock and fortress who will never fail to offer shelter.

Psalm 71:3 says *Be thou my strong habitation, whereunto I may continually resort: thou hast given commandment to save me; for thou art my rock and my fortress.*

The Shadow Of God's Wings

Have you ever been in a dark place late at night? There was no light. You didn't know the area. The wind was howling. You were all alone.

How did you feel? Probably afraid, at least a little bit.

Most of us aren't too eager to be in the shadows. Who knows what's out there? We fear the shadows because there is no light. We fear the shadows because of the unknown. We can't see ahead or around us. The last place we want to be is in a place filled with shadows.

Life has shadow times. Times when we don't know what is out there. Times when we don't know what is going to happen. Times when we can only imagine what we can't see. Times of trials and troubles and sadness.

We fear the dark times. We fear the unknown. We don't like the shadow times in life.

But let me tell you, there can be comfort and safety in the shadows. The shadows can be a place of shelter and an anchor for your soul if the shadow is the shadow of God's wings.

God knows that you face problems and trials. He loves you and He wants to be there for you during the hard times so He can spread His wings over you and protect you.

In the shadow of God's wings there is protection from the enemy, there is the comfort of God's presence, there is security in knowing you are not alone in your troubles. It is the safest place you can be. In life's roughest storms you can hide beneath the shadow of God's wings. There He will keep you safe.

I was amazed to find so many verses in the Bible that refer to riding on God's wings and to sheltering under His wings. Apparently God considers that an apt description for the place of safety which He offers to all who flee under His wings for protection and to those who ride on His wings and experience His power.

Exodus 19:4 says, *Ye have seen what I did unto the Egyptians, and how I bare you on eagles' wings, and brought you unto myself.*

Deuteronomy 32:9-11 says, *For the LORD'S portion is his people; Jacob is the lot of his inheritance.*

He found him in a desert land, and in the waste howling wilderness; he led him about, he instructed him, he kept him as the apple of his eye.

As an eagle stirreth up her nest, fluttereth over her young, spreadeth abroad her wings, taketh them, beareth them on her wings.

Ruth 2:12 says, *The LORD recompense thy work, and a full reward be given thee of the LORD God of Israel, under whose wings thou art come to trust.*

Psalm 17:8 says, *Keep me as the apple of the eye, hide me under the shadow of thy wings.*

Psalm 36:7 says, *How excellent is thy lovingkindness, O God! therefore the children of men put their trust under the shadow of thy wings.*

Safe in the Storm

Psalm 63:7 says, *Because thou hast been my help, therefore in the shadow of thy wings will I rejoice.*

Malachi 4:2 says, *But unto you that fear my name shall the Sun of righteousness arise with healing in his wings; and ye shall go forth, and grow up as calves of the stall.*

Psalm 91:4 says, *He shall cover thee with his feathers, and under his wings shalt thou trust: his truth shall be thy shield and buckler.*

The story is told of a farmer who had many acres of land. On his land he not only raised corn and wheat, he also had cows, horses, and chickens.

One spring a mother hen hatched a whole brood of baby chicks. Wherever she went, right behind her the little chicks would bob along in a straight line. They walked as fast as their little legs would carry them. They struggled to keep up with their mother so she wouldn't get too far ahead.

Whenever the mother hen became alarmed because of approaching danger, such as a nosey dog snooping around or a cow walking too close, she would call to her chicks and up she would raise her wings. All the chicks would gather under and huddle close. Then the mother hen would lower her wings over the entire brood of chicks. She would squat down low to the ground and cover her babies till the danger passed. Then up she would stand and up would go her wings and all the chicks would scatter when they saw the daylight.

One day, a great fire began on the farm. As hard as the farmer tired to put out the fire, he could not. Like the wind in a raging storm, the fire swept over the farm land burning everything in its path.

The mother hen sensed the danger and quickly called to her brood to gather close. Up went her wings and under ran all the chicks. Then the mother hen squatted down as close to the ground as she could.

Hours later, when the farmer was walking over his charred land, surveying the damage, he came upon the remains of the poor mother hen. With a sad heart the farmer reached down to lift the hen up.

To his surprise, out ran the little hen's entire brood of chicks. They survived the fire because their mother had given her life to keep her chicks close and safe under her wings.

Jesus' Wings

One day Jesus was speaking to his disciples and all the people who followed Him waited to hear His teachings. Jesus knew it wouldn't be long before they would take Him and crucify Him on the cross. He looked out over the city of Jerusalem and spoke of how He longed to gather and protect His people, just as a mother hen protects her brood, but they didn't want anything to do with Him.

In Matthew 23:37 Jesus said, *O Jerusalem, Jerusalem, thou that killest the prophets, and stonest them which are sent unto thee, how often would I have gathered thy children together, even as a hen gathereth her chickens under her wings, and ye would not!*

The people of Jesus' day rejected Him. Instead of running to Him for safety to hide under the shadow of His wings, they ran the other way. They nailed Him to a cross. They spit on Him and beat Him. They made fun of Him. Yet, Jesus still loved them. He still longed to gather them to Himself as a hen gathers her chicks. He was willing to give His life for them and for you, just to be able to offer an eternity in Heaven.

You may not have rejected His gift of salvation, but have you accepted His offer to shelter, safe and sound, under His wings? Do you find yourself running toward Jesus Christ or away from Him when your storms come up? In times of fear, confusion, and even anger you may find yourself running away from the shelter of His wings.

Don't. Even in the hard times, you can run under the shadow of His wings. You can talk to God and tell Him your needs. You can read your Bible and draw strength from His Word. You can be safe in the storm.

Perfectly Safe

When you turn to God to be your anchor, your shelter, the wings under which you nestle close, does that mean no harm will come to you? Yes. That is exactly what it means.

Don't get me wrong. It doesn't mean you will lead a storm free life. Or even that when you peek out after the storm the sky will have cleared completely and all clouds will be gone. I am not saying you will never suffer physical or even emotional pain. I am not saying life will be continually happy and peaceful. I am not saying God will make all your problems go away.

What I am saying is, yes, you will be under God's protection and nothing can happen to you that is not allowed by God. Nothing can happen that God does not have a purpose in allowing. You can know that if God allows a storm and its effects, then no eternal harm can ever come from it. You are perfectly safe.

What you view as harm is not viewed that way by God. What you think is terrible may be the very thing God uses to bring you great blessing. What you consider devastating may be the exact thing you need to make you more Christ-like.

After several years of fighting leukemia, I once heard Bo say, "If I could have the choice of having leukemia or not having it, I wouldn't change a thing."

Bo had learned that even though physical harm was coming to his body, a greater spiritual work was being done in his heart. He knew the cancer would most likely take his body and his life, but the things he had gained in exchange were of such lasting and spiritual value that it was all worth it. The harm being done to his body was temporary. It was not important. The eternal benefits he was reaping far outweighed all else.

As Bo sought shelter under the shadow of God's wings, he was perfectly safe. God was in control. God was doing what He needed to do for Bo's good and His glory. That was what was truly important.

2 Corinthians 4:15-18 says, *For all things are for your sakes, that the abundant grace might through the thanksgiving of many redound to the glory of God.*

For which cause we faint not; but though our outward man perish, yet the inward man is renewed day by day.

For our light affliction, which is but for a moment, worketh for us a far more exceeding and eternal weight of glory;

While we look not at the things which are seen, but at the things which are not seen: for the things which are seen are temporal; but the things which are not seen are eternal.

Can you be safe in the storm? Yes! Perfectly safe!

Calming Your Storm

- Make sure your place of shelter is a fortress, not a tent. Build on Christ the solid rock as your foundation in life. When you shelter in Him, nothing can harm you.

• Find your safety in God. Make sure you are tied securely to your anchor. Spend time daily with God in prayer and Bible study so that when the storms begin to rage, you will be securely tied to Jesus Christ, your anchor.

• During storms, nestle close under the shelter of God's wings. Experience the power of riding on top of God's wings. Don't run the other way when God invites you to take refuge under His wings. Know that is the safest place you can be. No matter what happens to your outward man, your inward man can be growing and maturing because of the storms you are enduring. You can be safe under His wings while experiencing His power as you ride on top of His wings.

• Sing songs that remind you that you are safe in Jesus Christ, such as, "Under His Wings," "The Solid Rock," "My Anchor Holds," "Wings As Eagles," "Rock of Ages," "Leaning on the Everlasting Arms," "From Every Stormy Wind," and more.

MEMORIZE THESE VERSES

Hebrews 6:19 *Which hope we have as an anchor of the soul, both sure and stedfast, and which entereth into that within the veil.*

Psalm 71:3 *Be thou my strong habitation, whereunto I may continually resort: thou hast given commandment to save me; for thou art my rock and my fortress.*

Psalm 57:1 *Be merciful unto me, O God, be merciful unto me: for my soul trusteth in thee: yea, in the shadow of thy wings will I make my refuge, until these calamities be overpast.*

Psalm 17:8 *Keep me as the apple of the eye, hide me under the shadow of thy wings.*

Comfort in the Storm

GARY'S STORM

Only people who know Gary and me extremely well know what I am about to tell you. Some people will be surprised to read this. It's not that it is such a deep, dark secret. It's just that when we traveled we chose not to share it with others so that our family life on the road would be as normal as possible.

In the chapter about courage I mentioned there was a period of time, before Gary and I were married, when Gary came home on a break from his traveling ministry. There was a reason he was off the road and at home.

When we traveled, people would ask us how many years we had been married. That was a question we were asked over and over during a week of meetings. It was a question we were not about to answer. We became quite good at changing the subject in such a way that people didn't realize we hadn't answered the question.

It wasn't quite so easy for me when I was with a group of women. They often began talking about one of their favorite subjects: childbirth. Someone would inevitably ask me about giving birth to Rynda. It escapes me why women love to talk about such private things, but I always replied, "It was a day at the beach."

That was the truth. On August 24th, the day Rynda was born, I was fifteen years old and I was enjoying a day at the beach at my parents' cottage. Rynda's birth mother, on the other hand, was on the other side of the state giving birth to my daughter.

In the early 1960's Gary had married a young lady he met in Bible college. Her name was Judy. Toward the end of their marriage Rynda was born. Then Judy became very ill. At first the doctors were puzzled. They thought she had some sort of severe arthritis that was causing her hands to become crippled. It came on fast and just kept getting worse. It wasn't long before Judy was not able to care for Rynda. Gary was soon changing diapers and caring for all of Rynda's needs. It became apparent something was terribly wrong with Judy. It wasn't arthritis.

One bad thing about life on the road is you can't go to your own doctor. You have to change doctors every week. As a result, a diagnosis was slow in coming. So they returned to Michigan to be near Gary's family and to find a doctor who could help. They also had some weeks of meetings that had been scheduled in that area.

One doctor finally found that Judy had a rare disease which was causing all the organs in her body to harden. The skin is an organ of the body, so the organ that first began to visibly show signs of trouble was her skin. They soon realized all of her internal organs were also showing signs of distress.

The doctor said the disease could progress slowly and take many years to run its course or it could move quickly. There was no way to tell. Either way, it was fatal.

So the little family went back to doing what God had given them to do. They began a week of meetings in a church and late one night Judy told Gary she thought she needed to go to the hospital. She was in extreme pain and was vomiting. Gary took her to the hospital.

After he had settled Judy for what was left of the night, Gary went back to the trailer. After praying, a calm came over him and he went to sleep.

A few hours later there was a knock on the trailer door. The pastor and his wife were there. They said they had gotten a call from the hospital and he needed to go there. The pastor's wife took Rynda, and Gary went with the pastor to the hospital.

They put Gary and the pastor in a room and a doctor came in to tell Gary in cold, hard terms that his wife had "expired." They had done all they could do but couldn't save her. Gary was in shock. At first he thought he was fine until the thought hit him that he had a twenty-two month old baby who didn't have a mother. He broke down.

The Lord had sent them to the right church because the pastor took over and began making vital decisions for Gary. The pastor canceled the rest of Gary's meetings for the year and made immediate arrangements for Gary and Rynda to return home. The pastor also talked to Gary's parents and told them people would tell them they should take Rynda from Gary and raise her. He warned them that Gary needed Rynda and they should not do that.

The pastor was right. Rynda was one of the only reasons he kept going. He felt he had lost everything but he knew he had to go on for her. He needed her to give him a purpose in life right then.

So Gary hooked up his trailer, gathered his daughter, and headed back to his home town.

Gary says that it felt like someone had reached down and ripped his heart out of his body. He was without a wife and his daughter was without a mother. He was hurting worse than he ever had before in his life.

In the months that followed, people would ask, "How are you doing?" he would reply, "I'm fine." They would say, "That's nice," and turn and walk away. He would scream within himself, "No, I am not fine. I feel like a giant hand has reached up inside me and ripped out my guts. I hurt, I ache, I am empty. You can go back to your spouse. I go to an empty trailer."

The only words that helped him were when people said, "I'm praying for you." That helped because he knew God knew what he needed and if they were talking to God about him, then God would give him what he needed.

Gary wondered what God was trying to tell him. Had he done something wrong? Was God throwing him out of the ministry? What should he do now? Gary says the only thing that kept him from being discouraged was the solid belief that God was in control and that He had a purpose. He couldn't begin to understand that purpose, but he just trusted God to do what was right.

Shortly after, the pastor of our home church asked Gary to take over Junior Church as a ministry while he was deciding what God wanted him to do.

It was months later in Junior Church that Gary and I got to know each other. We began working together and Gary taught me how to work with puppets. It was there that Gary began to see God wasn't through with him, He just had a different direction for him to go.

I had graduated from high school when I was seventeen and was in Cosmetology school at the time. I was also wondering what God wanted to do with my life. As a young teen I felt God wanted me to be a missionary or something like that. I wasn't sure what. Looking back I can clearly see why God didn't lead me to a Bible college after high school. I needed to be home so I could get to know Gary.

Rynda was just a little thing. Not quite three years old when Gary and I were married. On August third, at the age of eighteen, I became an instant mother, wife, and evangelist's wife. And I must admit, at times the whole thing was rather overwhelming.

When we started on the road together, I was too young to share my husband with the memory of a first wife. I had noticed that when people found out I was not Rynda's birth mother, they watched us differently. They assumed I was the story book "wicked stepmother" it seemed.

Many people have very effective ministries based on their trials, but Gary and I agreed that God did not intend for our ministry to be about sharing, week after week, about how Gary had lost his first wife. Our ministry was entirely different and we felt the past should stay in the past. So we didn't tell others. I was too young to handle it and Gary was still very sensitive. We decided that we were a family. While I may not have given birth to Rynda, she is mine. On that we three have always agreed.

So, we deflected questions about my age and how long we had been married. It was the only way to avoid having to repeat all the gory details every time someone asked. After all, we couldn't just say, "Yes, Rynda is five and we've only been married three years," or "I'm twenty and Rynda is five. And by the expression on your face I can tell you've just figured out I had to have been fourteen when I was married," or "No, Gary and I weren't married when Rynda was born." Any of those statements would have been grounds for kicking us out of a church for meetings if we didn't go on with a full explanation. Though none of them were true, words like: teen pregnancy, out of wedlock, and divorce would have raced through minds. So we kept our secret.

For years Gary wondered why God had allowed him to lose his first wife. What was the purpose? God could have allowed him to wait for me. We were from the same town and church. Why allow him to go through such agony?

We also knew the Lord didn't intend for us to minister to others with this tragedy. If the Lord had led Gary to use it to help others in our meetings, then he would have understood why it happened, but we clearly did not feel that was what God wanted. So he quit trying to figure it out and left it in God's hands.

On July 19, 2003 Gary began to understand. That was the day when Rynda lost Bo. Thirty years earlier, almost to the exact day, Judy had died. Gary had been thirty-one years old. Rynda was thirty-one years old. The similarities were amazing in many ways.

Nothing others said seemed to provide much comfort to Rynda at first. But one day Rynda looked at Gary and said, "You understand. You went through almost the exact same thing. You understand!"

Gary had his answer. One purpose for his storm was so that someday he would be able to help and comfort his very own daughter. When he talked to her and offered advice about what she was going through, she accepted it because he understood.

Sometimes we are at a total loss to understand why something has happened, but later, looking back, we can see God allowed it so we could be of help and comfort to someone else who needs our help.

II Corinthians 1:3-4 says, *Blessed be God, even the Father of our Lord Jesus Christ, the Father of mercies, and the God of all comfort; Who comforteth us in all our tribulation, that we may be able to comfort them which are in any trouble, by the comfort wherewith we ourselves are comforted of God.*

Trouble Accepting Aid?

Gary and I spent almost 30 years on the road. We learned to be alone with only each other for company. We were and are best friends. For the most part, Gary and I are both loners. We are that way by our natures.

Unlike the stereotype back-slapping evangelist and his perfectly at ease wife, Gary and I are both introverts. We have learned to be with strangers, but it's not comfortable for us. We are both most comfortable around people we know well. Yet, for years we met and talked with hundreds of people a week, but it was all so surface. We knew that in a few days we would hook up our trailer and leave.

Actually, we did build some very wonderful relationships over the years. We have friends that we met and for some reason we clicked with them. With those people we sought times to be together beyond our week in their church. Some friends are ministry friends who understand our needs. Some are church people who have reached beyond the boundaries of politeness and made true friends with us.

It isn't that people didn't care about us or that we didn't care about them, it was just that it was almost impossible for us to build a lasting relationship in five days. Very few people ever truly got to know us. Gary used to share my testimony in one of his messages about how shy I was as a teenager. I have had people say to me afterwards, "You're not an introvert. You were never shy!" That was how well people knew me. . . or didn't know me.

I admit, I did seem outgoing to those people. I learned to be outgoing as a means of self-preservation. I learned to stand on the platform and speak with apparent ease. I learned techniques for talking to people I didn't know. I learned to seem at ease in a crowd. But I never was. Not totally.

Gary is quiet and he doesn't enjoy people. He doesn't dislike people. He just doesn't like small talk or commotion. A noisy room makes it hard for him to think. It befuddles him. He's a sweet guy. He enjoys being with people he knows if it's in a small group. He and I can talk nonstop at times. But we can also be totally quiet for long stretches of time and not feel the need to fill the silence.

As a result, we find it hard to reach out to others that we don't know well. When Bo got sick and we came upon some real needs beyond ourselves, we were not quick to seek comfort from others. So, there were times when I felt all alone in my storm. It seemed like no one else really understood our hurt and sorrow.

It was my own fault. I had a hard time reaching out. We hadn't been settled in South Carolina for long at the time and we were still on the road some of the time. We still felt new in our church and people didn't know us well. So when others inquired about Bo, I put on a brave face and smiled. I gave a report of what was happening, but I don't think I ever said, "You can't believe how much this hurts! I don't know if I can handle it much longer!"

Never Let Them See You Sweat

I think one of the things that made me feel lonely and comfortless when it came to others was that everyone else seemed to handle their problems so much better than I felt I was. And that wasn't acceptable to me. After all, I was the evangelist's wife. I was the one others came to with their problems. Surely I could handle my own storms.

It seemed to me that others who were dealing with storms had a better grip on things. They never really seemed shaken by their problems. Maybe they went home, curled into balls and cried their hearts out in their beds too. I don't know. All I know is that I felt alone amongst my fellow Christians at times.

My biggest problem was feeling so helpless and so hurt. My heart ached. The pain was crippling at times. It made me feel like I wasn't trusting God if I couldn't just keep smiling instead of wanting to cry all the time.

Occasionally others added to that feeling. One lady asked me how I was holding up, then she basically added in an abrupt manner, "Well, you're a Christian, so keep a stiff upper lip!" or words to that effect. I felt as if I was being chastised for my fear and grief. This reinforced my notion that others would look down on me if I admitted anything less than complete joy, peace, and trust. I couldn't help but wonder, "If it were her son, could she keep a stiff upper lip?"

But I felt others expected me to keep a stiff upper lip, so I did my best. I held in all the fear and feelings of loneliness. I knew I wasn't the only one in the world whose kids were facing cancer, but it felt that way sometimes. I didn't know how to ask for help without having someone look down their nose at me.

Looking back, I wish I had not worried about those few who felt that way. I wish I had reached out to those who would have shown understanding and compassion. But I didn't look beyond what I perceived everyone else to be thinking.

I think sometimes Christians feel they shouldn't show any sign of weakness. They think they would be viewed by others as a spiritual failure. After all, we know a good Christian smiles through every woe and is never discouraged, right?

Wrong. As much as we wish we were, we aren't perfect. We are not superhuman. Life shocks, frightens, and confounds a Christian as much as any other human. If we can find the ability to smile and if we can keep our courage when surrounded by a storm, it is only because of the power and grace of God.

There are days you will find yourself pleading with God to help you because you don't have it in you to face your storm or find victory. That's okay. That's what God wants. He wants you to admit you don't have what it takes to make it through the storm. He wants you to turn to Him.

If someone looks down on you for not being perfect, then pray for that person. They need it more than you do. They apparently don't realize how difficult life's storms can be. When they confront one, if they are depending on their own superior coping powers, then they will be floundering also.

God knows you are weak. That's no surprise to Him. But He tells us in 2 Corinthians 12:9, *And he said unto me, My grace is sufficient for thee: for my strength is made perfect in weakness. Most gladly therefore will I rather glory in my infirmities, that the power of Christ may rest upon me.*

COMFORT FROM OTHERS

I can think back now and realize that there were many who truly did try to offer comfort. They didn't seem to think I had to be some type of super-Christian. There were friends who always asked how Bo was doing. They always said they were praying. That was a comfort.

One day when my mother was dying, I was having a particularly hard time handling watching her suffer. I remember walking out in the woods behind our house and telling God, "God, I need some help! I can't handle this!"

I walked into the house and the phone rang. It was the young lady who was my prayer partner that year. I didn't tell her how much I needed her call at that moment, but just praying together was such a comfort. I felt God had answered my plea for help.

On another day my friend Kay, who had been an emergency room nurse, called to say she was coming to visit Mom. Mom was totally out of it. I didn't realize it, but she had less than a day to live at that time.

When Kay got to the house I took her in to see Mom. The last time Mom responded to anyone was to Kay. Then she went back to sleep and never woke again. I suppose Kay took one look at Mom and realized that the end was very near. Kay helped me to arrange Mom's bed so that she would be the most comfortable. She raised the head a bit saying Mom would be able to breathe and swallow better that way.

When Kay left, I felt comforted. Looking back, her visit gave me confidence that I was doing everything possible for Mom at the time. God used her kindness to comfort me.

When Bo was so sick I remember that my pastor's wife would inquire about how I was doing and I could tell by the look on her face that she meant, "How are you REALLY doing?" But I couldn't tell her how I was really doing. I didn't know her well and I was afraid it would seem like a weakness to say, "Not great. In fact, lousy. I'm scared and hurting like I've never imagined possible." So instead I said, "I'm fine."

But at times I would sit in church and a special solo would break my heart. Often the pastor's words of spiritual comfort in messages just melted my insides. I would lower my head and shake. I would fight to control myself so that I wouldn't sit there in church and cry. I stopped wearing mascara for the longest time because I never knew when the tears would start to flow.

I guess, looking back, I wasn't always willing to accept comfort from others because I didn't think anyone else understood. Everyone else seemed to handle their trials so effortlessly. I suppose I was afraid that if I admitted that sometimes I wasn't doing so well I would be considered a terrible Christian. Maybe that's what everyone thinks. Maybe we are all hurting inside when the tragic happens but are too afraid or too proud to admit it.

Regardless, I denied myself comfort that could have been a help to me. No one else can solve the problem or take away the trial, but they can offer words of comfort and that can be all you need to help you on your way. I believe now that God often channels comfort to us through His children.

I've also come to believe that it doesn't matter what others think. Get the help you need. Find a friend who doesn't think you are a spiritual wimp just because you are having a difficult time in your storm. Don't be too proud or too afraid to grab onto a hand that is extended toward you in kindness and comfort.

Accepting Help

Sometimes you need more than comfort from others to make it. Gary and I were more in need of emotional support, but Bo and Rynda needed so much more than just emotional support. And it amazed me to watch how God provided over and over. So many dear people stepped up with just the help they needed, just when they needed it.

Pastor John and the people at Community Bible Church in Easley, where Bo and Rynda were members, went above and beyond the call of duty. They gave again and again out of hearts of true love. They helped financially, spiritually, physically, and emotionally. Often they didn't ask what needed to be done, they just saw a need and met it.

My Dad took his riding mower over and left it at the kids' house. Dad and Gary often went to mow, but Bo liked to get out and do things if he was able. When Bo was too weak to mow the grass, men from the church also came and mowed and did other tasks around their home. One lady organized people to come sit with Bo in the hospital when he was so terribly sick which enabled Rynda to go home to shower or try to get in a few hours at her job. One couple took their car for a tune up and got them new tires.

Bo and Rynda's other friends stepped up also. One friend could always be counted on to do whatever odd job needed doing. She and her mother moved into their apartment for several days the first week that Bo was diagnosed. They watched over things and took the dog for regular walks. On another hospital stay she took Rynda to lunch and to a salon for a manicure. She and her husband helped in so may other ways during the four years Bo was ill.

Another friend brought lunch to Rynda every day during one hospital stay so they wouldn't have that added expense. She would call to ask Rynda what she wanted and the meal would be delivered hot and ready.

Another group of friends collected a big basket of goodies and things to occupy Rynda's time while she sat in the hospital watching over Bo. One friend found a cushion that fit on the chair Rynda slept on so she could be more comfortable at night.

Another friend was our quiet rock of stability as we planned the funeral. We fondly called her our "funeral coordinator." She kept a notebook and wrote down everything that needed to be done, all the people she needed to call, all the times of the appointments that had to be kept. She kept things running smoothly when we were all too befuddled to think.

Martha's Method

Martha, as in Mary and Martha from the New Testament, often gets a bad rap. We think that she was doing it all wrong. But Jesus didn't say that. He did say Mary had chosen the better thing by choosing to sit and listen to Him, but He didn't say Martha had done anything wrong. In fact, I am sure that Jesus enjoyed the hospitality of Martha's home many times.

If you are a Martha, that's okay. God made you that way for a purpose and He wants you to use your talents for His glory. While you need to be careful not to be so caught up in doing so much busy work for others that you miss the spiritual things in life, you also need to show God's love to others in a practical way. One perfect time to show God's love is when someone is in the midst of a storm. That is the time when help is truly needed and your nurturing skills are best put to use. If you are a Martha, your aid would be greatly appreciated, I'm sure.

When my mom was in the hospital, it was such a help when someone would drop off a casserole. That meant I could stay at the hospital with Mom and know my family at home had something to eat.

When Rynda was with Bo in the hospital, it was such a help when meals were brought to her or someone slipped her a couple of dollars so she could eat in the cafeteria. When Bo was home from the hospital but too weak to work, or his immunity was so low he couldn't go out, just having a friend drop by to mow was a huge help.

You don't have to be a Martha Stewart to be of help to someone in need. You don't need to spend lots of money or do anything elaborate to lend a hand. When someone is in need, if the Lord lays it on your heart to help in some practical way, then do your best for the Lord and don't hold back because you think someone else may do better.

The best way to meet needs in a helpful manner is to offer what you can do in a specific way and if the help is needed, set up a time to do it. We are often quick to say, "If there's anything I can do to help, let me know." Those are famous last words. That's because many people say they want to help but actually they just want to sound helpful. In reality they have no intentions of doing anything.

Instead, tell the person in need what you can do and be specific. Say, "I'd love to fix a meal for your family. When would that be convenient for you?" or "Can I come by on Saturday morning and mow your lawn?" or "Would it be helpful if I watched your kids sometime this week?" Ask if the skills you possess would be something that would be appreciated. If so, set up a definite time to do the job or bring the offered gift.

Be aware of what people need. You might want to ask a close friend or family member if your services would be needed. You could watch for needs that become apparent. Often just a small service can provide great comfort.

THE BIG BOO BOO SYNDROME

For those of you who wish to offer comfort to someone who is going through a storm. Let me offer a few suggestions. Let me also mention a few "No no's."

Every summer our church gives their Sunday School teachers a chance to take a short break. Summer substitute teachers are enlisted to fill the open positions. This summer Gary and I volunteered to teach the three year old class. These little guys are about as cute as they come. After a bit of play time we gather them all around to teach them a simple Bible verse, sing songs, and hear a short Bible story.

Last Sunday about eleven little ones were staring intently at me when something I said, I'm not quite sure what, reminded one of the little guys of his Boo Boo. He pulled up the cuff of his pants to show me a scuffed place with a small scab. That was just the beginning. Within seconds ten other little ones were searching diligently for Boo Boos on their body. Some began showing places that only a three year old could get away with displaying!

Fortunately for me, three year olds have the attention span of a gnat, so I was able to distract them and get back on track with my story. But I have found there is nothing a tiny tyke enjoys more than showing off his Boo Boos.

The same is true for adults. I call it "The Big Boo Boo Syndrome." Everyone seems to love to launch into great detail about their latest or most traumatic problem. The only difference is that they aren't quite so quick to show you the actual scars. Although I have had people offer to show me scars if I was interested. I wasn't.

The summer Gary's back ruptured, it seemed like everyone had a story about a ruptured disc or back surgery gone wrong that they wanted to share with us. Not one of their stories was comforting or encouraging.

"Oh! Don't let those doctors go operating on your back!" they'd say. "You'll never be the same! I had back surgery and I've walked with a limp ever since. Wanna see my scar?"

Comfort in the Storm

People told us the most discouraging stories. By the time we had an appointment to see the neurosurgeon, we were scared stiff!

But people will always make an attempt at words of comfort. The problem is often they have not thought about the effect those words will have on anyone else.

There was the man who chose to comfort Gary after the loss of his wife with these words, "I lost my first wife too. The Lord gave me another one. That feeling you had with the first wife will never be there with anyone else. It will never be the same. It will never be as good, but you'll find someone else."

Encouraging? Hardly. And I might add that guy was totally wrong. Gary actually found someone much better, if I do say so myself!

You would think people might be a tad more sensitive about telling horror stories to people with cancer or other life threatening illnesses, but they don't seem to be. One of Bo's friends stood by his bedside and declared, "My cousin had leukemia. He died."

Thanks for that news flash. Downright frightening!

I'm not sure what it is about telling horror stories to someone when you should be trying to comfort them, but apparently it's just human nature to want to tell how badly you've had it. One upmanship I suppose. And it's not just limited to physical horror stories. Any problem you may have is fair game.

After everyone did their best to frighten us about back surgery, which by the way went extremely well for Gary, I decided that I would keep my horror stories to myself. When Bo was facing his first bone marrow biopsy, I didn't mention to him that I had one done when I was in the seventh grade and it still stands out in my mind as one of the most painful things a doctor has ever done to me. I kept that morsel to myself.

Perhaps you are a person who loves to show off your Boo Boos. Please, in Christian love, stop and think before you speak. Remember, speak words that will provide comfort, not fear or discouragement.

Gary has said many times that the person who comforted him the most when his first wife died was the friend who didn't say a word, but merely put an arm around his shoulder and cried with him.

So should you say something? Unless you are very close to the person or truly have gone through the exact same trial, please don't say, "I know exactly how you feel." You don't. No one knows exactly how anyone else feels. No one but God.

But yes, I do think you should feel free to approach them and, with sensitivity, let them know you are thinking of them and praying for them. I do think it is always a comfort to know people care about you and that they are praying for you. Beyond that, there really isn't much you can do unless you know of a specific need with which you can help. But sometimes, just letting someone know you care may help them not to feel so all alone.

If you are the person going through the storm, keep in mind that no matter what horror story others may tell you, it may not be true. It may have gotten worse as the story is told and retold. What happened to the teller may have been worse when it happened to them fifty years ago, but times and procedures have improved.

There are times when you just don't need to hear more bad news. Even if it is true. Maybe it's the Yankee in me, but I don't think it would be rude if, when someone starts into a story you really don't need to hear, you just hold up a hand and sweetly say, "Please, don't tell me. I'll find out soon enough."

Lessons I Learned About Comfort

People mean well.

Truthfully, others don't always bring comfort. I do believe they intend to, but let's face it, when we speak to someone who is having a major storm, most of us are at a loss for words that will comfort. We all want to say just the right thing, but what is the right thing?

I know that when I see someone who is going through hard times, I hesitate to say anything. I wonder if I mention the problem or sorrow, that it will only make them feel worse.

Words can't change or fix things. But I have found there is comfort in the fact that people care enough to try to offer comfort, feeble as the attempt may be. What seems to bring the most comfort is the love and support they offer. Knowing someone cares somehow makes the storm more bearable.

People just don't always know what to say and sometimes they don't think before they speak. So give them the benefit of the doubt. They wouldn't bother at all if they didn't care about you. So repeat after me, "People mean well. People mean well. . ."

God's Word Gives Comfort.

Don't waste too much time searching for comfort in the words of others. You may find it, you may not. The only true words of comfort will be found in God's Word.

I found great comfort from God's Word. There were particular passages that I read over and over. They gave hope. They encouraged me. They let me know God understood and cared about what I was going through.

The Bible is such a wonderful source of comfort because it lets you know that your God is with you. He is strong, He is sympathetic, and it is a comfort to know He knows what is going on, even when you don't. He has all the answers even when you don't.

Gary and Rynda love to tease me about the way I comfort myself when I am sick and feeling particularly down. I sing, "Does Jesus Care?" Whenever I get sick Rynda will ask me, "Are you singing 'Does Jesus Care?' yet?" It just helps me to draw comfort. It helps remind me that, yes, Jesus does care!

About five months before Mom died, I caught a flu that turned into bronchitis. It dragged on for six weeks. Soon Gary and Mom were also sick. I would try to help Mom because she could do so little for herself, but I was so weak I could barely function. Rynda had her hands full with Bo. Dad and Gary helped as much as possible, but there were things only I could do for Mom. I seemed to spend quite a bit of time singing that song. I like to think of it as encouraging myself in the Lord as David did.

Encourage yourself with God's Word. It is a comfort to know God cares. It is a comfort to know He is always ready to lend a listening ear. It is a comfort to know He has gone through sorrow and hard times. He understands.

Hebrews 4:15-16 says, *For we have not an high priest which cannot be touched with the feeling of our infirmities; but was in all points tempted like as we are, yet without sin.*

Let us therefore come boldly unto the throne of grace, that we may obtain mercy, and find grace to help in time of need.

Psalm 119:50 says, *This is my comfort in my affliction: for thy word hath quickened me.*

God's Power Comforts.

Often in a storm you feel powerless and weak. But that's not a problem for God. He tells you He gives comfort by offering His power and strength when you have none of your own. Your weakness is an occasion for God to show His power. When you are without strength, God will be your strength. You can lean on Him and He will hold you up.

II Corinthians 12:9 says, *And he said unto me, My grace is sufficient for thee: for my strength is made perfect in weakness.*

God's Presence Comforts.

No one wants to go through a problem or trial alone. That is why, in the fieriest storm, when we feel all alone, we can know our God is beside us at all times. The Bible tells us He will never leave us. It tells us He will never forsake us. Through each storm in life until the final storm of death, God is always, always with us. That is comforting.

Psalm 23:4 says, *Yea, though I walk through the valley of the shadow of death, I will fear no evil: for thou art with me; thy rod and thy staff they comfort me.*

BE OF GOOD COMFORT

God will not leave you comfortless. He understands and He cares. Although He may allow a storm into your life, He is always close at hand to offer comfort. When you find yourself in need of comfort, turn to the One who is the God of all comfort.

Remember the woman in the Bible who had an issue of blood for twelve long years? She tried everything to solve her problem in life, but nothing helped. Her money was gone. None of the doctors could help her. She was an extremely discouraged woman. But one day she learned Jesus was coming to her town. She turned to Him for help. Jesus cured her. Then He told her to be of good comfort.

Maybe you also have become discouraged. You are badly in need of the kind of comfort only God can give. Good news! Just as Jesus Christ offered comfort to that woman, He offers you the same comfort. It's yours for the taking. Be of good courage because Jesus Christ will comfort you.

Luke 8:48 says, *And he said unto her, Daughter, be of good comfort: thy faith hath made thee whole; go in peace.*

Comfort in the Storm

CALMING YOUR STORM

• Accept comfort from others. Accept the help that is offered. If you need to, ask for help. Others are usually happy to find a practical way to help you. It is not a sign of weakness to need to lean on others now and then.

• Remember that people mean well. Be quick to forgive unkind or thoughtless words. You have bigger fish to fry. Instead, draw comfort from the fact that they cared enough to try to offer something, even if it didn't come out right.

• Draw on God's power. When you have no strength of your own, draw on God's strength. Just ask for it. When you are too weak to go any further, let God give you the strength to keep on doing what you must do. Lean on Him. His strength will hold you up.

• Draw comfort from God's Word. His words bring such comfort. When you feel like no one understands, you can know that God understands because His Word tells you He understands. When you feel all alone, you can know that God is with you because He tells you He is with you. When the words of others bring no comfort, know that God's Word always has the comfort you need.

• Sing songs that bring comfort. Here are a few: "Abide With Me," "Be Still My Soul," "Blessed Assurance," "Oh God, Our Help In Ages Past."

MEMORIZE THESE VERSES

Hebrews 13:5b *I will never leave thee, nor forsake thee.*

II Corinthians 1:3-4 *Blessed be God, even the Father of our Lord Jesus Christ, the Father of mercies, and the God of all comfort; Who comforteth us in all our tribulation, that we may be able to comfort them which are in any trouble, by the comfort wherewith we ourselves are comforted of God.*

Luke 8:48 says, *And he said unto her, Daughter, be of good comfort: thy faith hath made thee whole; go in peace.*

The Passing of the Storm

DAMAGE CONTROL

There comes a time when every storm passes. It's done. There will be more storms in the future, but this one is gone. Now what?

You probably know that just because the storm has passed, it really isn't over. Now is the time to grieve and to heal. It is important that you do just that. As much as we would like to just sweep everything under the rug and pretend it doesn't exist, it does exist. There was a storm and it's time to clean up before you can truly move on.

I want to be very cautious about what I say in this chapter. I am not a counselor. I have no formal training that would allow me to help someone through this difficult and painful time of the storm's aftermath. I can only tell you what I have experienced and what has seemed to help me and my family.

EVERY STORM LEAVES ITS MARK

Winter in South Carolina, where I now live, is normally mild and it doesn't often stay cold for long periods of time. We do occasionally get some nasty weather. When I lived in Michigan I was never surprised to see snow fall in the early winter months and it would stay with us until the first thaw the following spring. But winter in the south comes in short blasts. If there is snow on the ground, it's not likely to be around for more than a few days at a time. Most often the snow will melt by the next day when the temperature rises.

The Eye of the Storm

My first snow storm in South Carolina was quite a revelation for this former Yankee. It amazed me how quickly everything shut down at the slightest sign of snow. Though I've come to understand the attitude toward snow down here, it baffled me at first.

The impact of a Southern snow storm usually starts the day before it actually hits. The weather forecasters and even the news anchors will lead with the top story being about the impending snow storm. They will show the storm on Super Doppler as it approaches and warn of its coming in somber tones.

The next thing to happen is everyone rushes out to buy milk and bread. That's an important part of the process, believe me. The store shelves, which formerly contained milk and bread, are empty within a few hours. Even at the Super Wal-Mart. Honest!

I never have figured out why everyone buys milk and bread. If I were convinced we were actually going to be socked in by a storm for more than a few days, I'd see the sense in buying milk and bread. But knowing that it's more apt to be several hours, I'd rather have pizza and Pepsi. Milk and bread just don't appeal to me. But that's what everyone rushes out to buy.

Then the snowflakes begin to drift gently down. The first time it happened after we moved here, I was expecting a doozy of a storm after all the hype. I woke up and peeked out my window with the expectation of seeing a foot of snow on the ground. Instead there was a light dusting of snow on the ground and a few flakes swirling around in the air. That was it.

I assumed the storm had gone in another direction and missed us completely. But no, this was the storm. I turned on the TV and the weather caster, who broke into the programing about every half hour, assured us the storm had hit. Across the bottom of the screen they ran a ticker tape message telling which schools and businesses were closed, which was all of them apparently. Greenville had shut down completely. I was baffled.

For the better part of two days, all Greenvillians stayed home. The next day the snow appeared to be gone, but everything was still closed. The reporter explained that the roads were slick and everyone should stay home. About ten o'clock the temperature rose into the low fifties and the snow melted completely. The ticker tape began notifying us that schools would open the next day, second shifts of work for businesses were now open, and night classes at Greenville Tech were going to be held.

The Passing of the Storm

I could just picture everyone in Greenville dipping their bread in their milk as they watched the broadcast. I called Tony's Pizza.

In Michigan we wouldn't have blinked an eye at those few flakes. We trudged to work or school with several feet of snow on the ground for months on end and never gave it a second thought.

But in defense of my now beloved South, there is a good reason everything shuts down. They don't have the equipment to handle the snow like they do in the North. Besides, Southerners are smart. Why not stay home and enjoy a day or two of relaxation and frolicking in the snow, what there is of it?

After all, winter comes in such short spurts, you might as well enjoy it. Everyone I know down here looks forward to a few days when the snow starts to fly. They know everything will shut down and everyone will stay home for a day or two to enjoy making snowballs and sipping cocoa by the fireside.

I don't make fun of Southerners' anymore. I'm one of them now and I totally agree with their way of looking at snowflakes. I must admit. I love those snow days. I don't have to feel guilty for taking time off and reading a favorite book or pulling out some games to play. I know our office building is located only a few steps away in our back yard, but why work? If all of Greenville can play hookey, so can I. But I still prefer pizza and Pepsi.

While we Southerners may enjoy the snow days, no one I know looks forward to an ice storm. Ice storms can be very nasty down here and they do great damage. We get more ice than snow in Greenville. Often it will start out as rain and the temperature will start to drop. The rain turns to ice and we watch in dread as the roads become impassable and the trees begin to bend under the tremendous weight of the ice on laden limbs.

Our house is surrounded by trees and we always keep a close eye on them. We don't want one to come through the roof one day. We bundle up and go take a survey of what is happening around the yard. We'll grab low limbs and shake them, but that is rarely enough to do any good. It's not unusual to lose six or seven trees in an ice storm. They will bend until they snap in two and it sounds like a shotgun being fired.

Yet the impassable roads and damaged trees are only part of the problem. As the trees bend and snap, they take down power lines. Then we lose power. Many people go to stay in motels or with family in other areas. Last winter one ice storm caused such damage that there were people in our area without power for almost two weeks. That is miserable and costly. It can also do some major damage to streets and homes.

Eventually it warms up. As the ice finally melts, everyone begins to survey the damage. They do their best to haul downed limbs to the sides of the roads and saw whole tree trunks into manageable pieces. The power company has trucks everywhere trying to restore power. It's a mess.

Even though the storm has passed, there is still lots to be done. Life does not go back to normal until the clean up is accomplished. And that takes time.

The same is true with your storms. When they pass, you are relieved, but you may find that you still have clean up to do before your life can return to normal. Clean up is never easy and it can take plenty of time and effort.

It takes time to grieve your losses. It takes time to heal. It takes time for life to return to normal. But time does tend to heal.

The Grieving Process

Bo would go home from the hospital whenever possible and he tried to stay home as long as he could. There were entire months when he would be in remission. But he didn't stay that way long and the outpatient chemo treatments would begin again. Then the time would come when Bo and Rynda both knew it was time to go back to the hospital.

In the fall of 2002 Bo came out of remission and started a new type of chemo. Early the following Spring he became very sick. Instead of getting better, he was getting worse. He was admitted to the hospital and the doctors began to search for the problem. It wasn't the leukemia. What they found was a second cancer. The new type of chemo had given Bo lymphoma. Now he had to contend with two types of cancer.

The doctors were baffled. The chemo that caused the lymphoma was the same one they normally used to cure it. As they frantically searched for answers, Bo got sicker and weaker. He slept most of the time and he looked terrible. There was a point when we all felt he would be gone soon. But he pulled through. He regained some strength and went home.

From the new books that Rynda had handed me to read, I could tell that although lymphoma is curable in the first two stages, everything pointed to the fact that Bo was most likely in the fourth stage. I kept that piece of information to myself. He seemed to feel stronger and I knew

The Passing of the Storm

God's timing is not ours. Bo seemed to be doing better and that was good enough for us.

It was a Tuesday afternoon in July of 2003 when Rynda called to ask me to come meet them at the hospital. They were taking Bo back in. I drove to the hospital and met them in the lobby. Rynda went into the business office to attend to some paperwork. I took Bo up to his room in his wheelchair.

The nurse told us which room he would be in and we headed that way. With his jeans and shirt still on, he climbed onto the bed and we began to chat. He looked so normal. Well, normal except he had no hair from the last type of chemo he had been given and except for the fact that his fingernails were actually blue. He looked pretty weak too.

We chatted about mundane things. Rynda and Bo had always been so careful not to dwell on the cancer. It's not that they pretended it didn't exist, they just didn't want to give in to believing he couldn't be healed. They wanted to keep things as normal as possible. So they didn't give in. They kept trusting that God would do what was best for them.

Bo and I chatted about the trip to Oregon that my dad and I were scheduled to take in a couple of days. The year before, Bo and Rynda had gone with us and we had a wonderful time with my brother and his family.

All of a sudden Bo looked at me and said, "They said the cancer has spread to my liver."

I was a bit stunned. I didn't know what to say. He had brought it up so abruptly. "Yes, that's what Rynda told me on the phone."

"It doesn't sound good, does it?" Bo asked. I looked into his eyes. He seemed to know that whether or not he talked about it, his cancer was really bad and it wasn't ever going to get better.

All I could say was, "No."

Then Bo changed the subject and we talked about other things. I feel like it was Bo's way of saying to me, "I know how bad this is."

Rynda got back to the room. The nurse came and I stepped out as Bo changed into a gown. Then the nurse gave Bo medication to help with the pain for the bone marrow biopsy they were about to perform. Soon he was drowsy.

That was the last real conversation I had with Bo. He was pretty out of it after that. All day Wednesday I stayed with Rynda and we chatted, but Bo just slept. By Thursday morning my dad and I were on a plane to Oregon. When my brother met us at the airport that night he told me Rynda wanted me to call her right away. Bo was in intensive care and things looked very bad.

Friday was spent getting an emergency flight home. We flew out on Saturday morning. Late that evening, when our plane touched down on the return trip, Dad spotted Gary and Rynda waiting for us. The instant Dad said they were at the airport, instead of at the hospital, I knew Bo was gone. Rynda would never have left Bo's side otherwise. He had died about the same time our flight took off from Oregon that morning. I like to think that at the moment we were lifting off of the runway, Bo was lifting off for his eternal home.

Rynda had always bathed Bo while he was in the hospital. That final day was no exception. Rynda stayed in the room to help the nurses as they prepared Bo to be taken away. She gave him one last bath. The last thing she could do for him.

Medical personnel on the cancer floor don't often attend funerals. It would be too depressing. But at Bo's funeral there were four rows filled with doctors and nurses, along with employees who mopped the floors and brought food trays. There were so many technicians from the diagnostic center in the hospital who wanted to be there that it was decided to shut the center down for the day so everyone who worked there could attend the funeral. They came as a tribute to a man whose kind words and thankful heart had touched their lives and made an impact for God.

It can be hard to be thankful or joyful when times are hard or things aren't going our way. We wonder why this is happening to us. But oh, what an impact a life can make for Christ when others see a kind and thankful spirit demonstrated, especially in the hard times!

Because Jesus Wept

After Gary's first wife died, someone sent him a tract which said instead of grieving and having a funeral, a Christian should have a home going party. It should be a time of joy and celebration. It said Christians should not grieve. I say, the person who wrote that tract either never lost a loved one or they were deep into stage one of denial! If you truly feel that way, more power to you, but it is not wrong to grieve.

I'll admit, there are definitely times when death is a relief and a joy. When the person is a Christian and they have suffered long or are well

The Passing of the Storm

advanced in years, then it can be a happy occasion. It is a joy to know your loved one is with the Lord. But just because the dear departed one is happy in Heaven does not mean that those left behind do not miss them and should not grieve. If you loved the person, you will miss them. The grieving period is for the one who suffered the loss, not for the one who has gone on. You know the one who has gone is better off with the Lord. You know they are no longer in pain. That brings tremendous comfort, yet while they are home with the Lord, you are still here on earth. Alone. No matter how happy you may feel for your departed loved one, it still hurts to lose them. It does!

While Rynda was thankful Bo was no longer suffering, she was a young widow and she was in great pain. It was important that she mourn.

I believe God understands our need to mourn. His Word tells us there is a proper time to weep and mourn. Nowhere does it say Christians should never mourn.

Ecclesiastes 3:4 says, *A time to weep, and a time to laugh; a time to mourn, and a time to dance.*

Jesus certainly understood grief. When His good friend Lazareth died, Jesus wept. I have heard some say He was just crying because Mary and Martha had such weak faith to not believe He would raise their brother. But I don't believe that. I think Jesus was experiencing a truly human feeling called grief.

Never before had God experienced grief in the same way we humans do. But now, Jesus did understand grief. He could feel what it was like to lose someone He loved. Sure, He knew Lazareth was in Glory. He even knew that in a few minutes Lazareth would be well and walking around again. But for that moment, He truly understood what you and I feel when we lose someone we dearly love.

Because Jesus wept, we know that it is not unChrist-like to weep also.

Isaiah 53:3a is talking about Jesus when it says, *He is despised and rejected of men; a man of sorrows, and acquainted with grief.*

"Okay," some say, "What about the verse that says we shouldn't sorrow." The Bible never says not to grieve. It says we shouldn't sorrow in the same way as someone who has no hope. An unsaved person has no hope of ever seeing their loved one again. They can see no purpose in death. Death is a final, senseless, and painful thing to them.

It's different for a Christian. You aren't to grieve on and on with no hope of ever seeing your loved one again. You do have hope! You will see your loved one again in Heaven!

That helps you to face the pain and sorrow in a different manner than those with no hope. It helps you to see your loss from an entirely different perspective. But it does not mean you shouldn't grieve.

I Thessalonians 4:13 says, *But I would not have you to be ignorant, brethren, concerning them which are asleep, that ye sorrow not, even as others which have no hope.*

It's okay to grieve. In fact, I think it is healthy to grieve. I think it is necessary in order to go on with a productive life. It is necessary to going on to be effective for God.

People around you may try to stop you from grieving. The reason they do is most likely it hurts them to see you suffer. They mean well. But they need to understand grief is a natural process and it must be done for healing to occur. An open wound must be cleansed so healing can begin. If the cleansing effects of grief do not occur, the wound will not heal but will continue to fester.

You may even find yourself trying to avoid grief. It certainly isn't a pleasant emotion. I felt for quite a long time that I couldn't grieve because I needed to be strong for Rynda and because I had so many other responsibilities. So I held it all inside. I put it off. It was a long time after Bo had passed on before I faced the fact that I needed to grieve before I could begin the healing process. When I finally allowed grief to do it's work, healing began. Little by little I did heal.

THE AMAZING VANISHING PERSON

One thing that often happens while you are grieving is that others feel they should never mention your loved one again. Perhaps you would rather not talk about them. That is fine. But most grieving people have a need to go over the good times and discuss the things that are swirling around in their mind about the final days. Most grieving people find it disconcerting when it seems like no one even seems to remember that their loved one ever existed. Of course others remember, but they feel you would be hurt if they mentioned them.

In truth, you most likely would find comfort in being able to talk about your loved one. You may not want total strangers or people who aren't close to you trying to make you talk about them, but with friends you do want to talk.

Find a friend who understands your need to share stories and memories. It doesn't have to be all the time, but just talking about your loved one now and then, as you feel like it, can be a big part of the grieving process.

Sixty-Seven Stars

My mother passed away in August of 2001. It was a sad thing, but also a relief. She was no longer in pain. She was with the Lord.

When I asked Dad if he wanted to move back into the master bedroom since the hospital bed had been removed, he said he preferred that the room be returned to how it had been when Mom was alive, but he wanted to stay in the guest room. He had settled there and he was happy.

I went through Mom's closet and drawers looking for medicines and other things that needed to be discarded. But that was all. There was no rush. I left her clothes hanging in the closet and folded in the drawers. I didn't have the heart to do anything yet. Somehow the thought of throwing away her things felt to me like we would be throwing Mom away. Gary and I put the bed back in place. We covered it with the pink chenille spread that Mom had loved and put all her fancy crocheted dolls on top. Everything looked just as it had when Mom was alive. We pulled the door shut.

In December when it came time to decorate the Christmas tree, I decided to look in Mom's closet to see if I could find some things I thought were stored on the top shelf. As I pulled a chair up to begin my search, I noticed a box on the closet floor that I had not noticed before. It was sitting out in the open. Strange I had not seen it before. In bold letters on the top of the box was my name in my mom's handwriting. It said, "This box belongs to Wendy."

I picked up the box and wondered what on earth was inside. As I lifted the lid I saw a small note with my name laying on top of some folded tissue paper. I lifted the note and opened the tissue paper. Inside lay red and green and white beaded stars Mom had hand made. There were sixty-seven stars, all in the colors I had requested at an earlier time. I had forgotten all about asking for those stars, but Mom apparently hadn't.

I opened the note and it simply said, "Wendy, I love you. Mom."

I couldn't believe it. I had been missing Mom, especially around Christmas time. Mom always loved Christmas. She would decorate the house and she always insisted that the tinsel on the tree be hung just right. She always made hundreds and hundreds of fancy cookies and would put them on plates to share with all her friends. This year, with Mom missing, everything seemed so quiet and empty.

Then I found the stars. I was so touched to receive one last Christmas gift from my mom. I got in the car and drove to the cemetery. I sat on her grave and cried my heart out. I knew Mom was happy with the Lord, but I missed her. And I was so touched the Lord had allowed me to find that box just at the time I needed it most.

The Healing Process

One interesting thing is that even though I have been working on this book for a couple of months, it is today, July 19, 2006, that I have begun to work on this chapter that deals with July 19, 2003, the day Bo died. It was not by my design, but the subject is near to my heart today.

As I examine my feelings now, on the third anniversary of Bo's death, I find that even though I still miss Bo, I have healed quite a bit. I didn't think I ever would. Time truly does help. But I know I will always miss Bo, no matter how much time elapses. And that's fine with me.

I have cried quite a bit as I have written about the things we went through. Writing about it has stirred up many old feelings, and when I recall them, they still feel as fresh and painful as they did at the time they occurred. But it's not exactly the same now as then. I can look at it all with different eyes. I see what I could not see then. I see how faithful God has been each step of the way. Through the storm, God never let us down. He never left us. He never failed us. And even when things looked the darkest, God was working for our good.

Gary and I moved in with Rynda immediately after Bo died. The first several nights I slept right by her side in their big king size bed. It was an extremely hard time for Rynda. The first night when she walked into their bedroom she took one look at the room and I could see the impact it had on her. That morning she had left Bo in the hospital and now she was returning home without him. That was something she had never done in the past four years. She had always stayed in the hospital

The Passing of the Storm

with him but now he would never return home. She bowed her head and began to cry. I just held her.

We stayed for about six weeks. Slowly she began to regain her emotional strength. She began to get her footing. When we felt she was ready to face life in her home alone, we finally went home.

Soon after we moved out, Rynda found a sweet Christian young lady to be her roommate. The Lord sent just the right person to be with Rynda. It was a relief to know she wouldn't be all alone in the house at night and she would have someone to talk to and spend time with. Life moved on. Rynda began to heal.

Awhile later Rynda informed us she had met a nice young man. She had known him for years. He had been a friend of Bo. They had know each other in passing, but she was just beginning to get to know him better now. His name was Stephen. Slowly we began to see Rynda smile again.

At first we worried about Rynda moving on so quickly. But we also realized that Rynda had done much of her grieving during the last few months of Bo's life. In the Spring he had been extremely sick. He had almost died. She vaguely discussed funeral arrangements with us then and from that time on Rynda truly understood that it wouldn't be long. Rynda said there were times she would lay her head on his bed and cry. If Bo realized she was crying, she said he would reach out a hand and place it on her head. They both knew it wouldn't be long.

So, much of her grieving was done early, before Bo passed on. And Rynda was young. She needed to move on. She loved Bo with all her heart, but she had mourned for four years while he was fighting the cancer. She was ready to move on after several months of mourning had passed. Gary and I began to adjust to the idea that Rynda needed to move on. It was hard at first, but what joy it was to see her happy again!

Stephen and Rynda were married the following year in September. He is truly a Godsend. I had prayed for so long that Rynda would not crumble under the pain and pressure of losing Bo. The Lord answered my prayers in the form of Stephen.

Stephen is a joy. He is funny and bright. He understands what we have all gone through and takes it with grace. Today, July 19, he took the day off from the deli he owns to be at home with Rynda.

When the Lord took Bo, I could not imagine how Rynda would ever be able to face life without him. Bo was a joy to us. He was all we could ever have asked for in a son-in-law. I surely couldn't imagine how any other man could be what Rynda needed.

But for as wonderful and as loving as Bo was, I now believe he was not as well suited to Rynda as Stephen is. I could not see that at the time. I did not need to see that at the time. But I see it clearly now.

We still love Bo deeply, as we would our own son, but in so many ways, Stephen is a more suitable mate for Rynda. And we thank God for doing all that He has done in His own time and His own way.

God, in His wisdom, knew what Rynda needed, when she needed it. Stephen has been a comfort to us all. He is accepting of our need to work through our pain and loss. He has brought joy and fun back into our family. And he is a faithful Christian husband who makes our daughter happy and secure.

DIFFERENT FOR EVERYONE

The healing process occurs at all different times for people. Everyone is different and losses are different. For most of Rynda's less than six year marriage to Bo, they waited on the inevitable. The last four years were filled with cancer and hospitals. It was a hard road with a hard end. But in a way, that made it much easier for her to move on. That, and watching someone you love suffer, makes it easier to let go too. You want them to be out of pain. When they are finally at peace, you are relieved and happy for them.

But not everyone is ready to move on so quickly. You may feel like people are pushing you to "get over it." They want you to feel better and move on. But moving on is different for everyone. And it can be very difficult also.

I do think that if you have grieved and not held it all in, it will be easier to move on. But I also think you shouldn't be pushed to move on. Healing will come in its own time. And that time is different for everyone.

If it has been a long process for you and healing never seems to come, then maybe you need to get some professional help. If you haven't been able to face getting out of bed and dressing for two years, then you should seek help from your pastor or a good Christian counselor. I have found that grieving lessens with time. Pain lessens as you allow God to apply healing to your heart. If that isn't the case for you, you may need to seek help. It would be a wise thing to do.

Make It Worthwhile

Part of the healing process for me has been to write about Bo and all that happened. The writing began in my diary. Then I wrote a story for my Children's Church materials about Bo's Blessings Book. Now I am writing this. And I am finding that God is using it to heal my heart.

Gary found a way to remember and honor Bo in his ministry. For years we had a potter's wheel that sat unused. Gary meant to dig it out some day and use it for a message on "The Potter and the Clay." After Bo became so sick, he finally did just that. He worked on his message and now he presents it in churches all over our area. He carefully compares the pottery process to the work God does in the life of a Christian.

When Gary talks about going through the fire, he explains that a vessel can either blow apart because of a hidden flaw or they can come out more beautiful and useful. He tells Bo's story and shows how Bo was tried in the furnace of affliction and when he came out his life was a beautiful testimony for God.

You may find your own way to honor your loved one and begin your healing process. Maybe you want to use your experiences to help others who are going through tough times. Maybe you want to create some sort of memorial that will be a blessing to you and to others. Not necessarily a "shrine" to your loved one, but something in their memory that will bring glory to God.

Reaching out to others is a healthy and productive way to heal. I believe it can be honoring to God and a wonderful testimony to use your storm to aid someone else in some way. Finding ways to pass on the things you have learned in the storm can add value. It can also be of great help to others and it can be a testimony of God's grace in your life.

Moving On

One trip the people left behind often take is a guilt trip. Guilt keeps you from moving on and healing. Maybe you feel guilty about what happened. You wonder, "Did I do enough?" "Could I have stopped this?" "What if I had been there?" "What if . . ."

You mustn't play "If history." You mustn't torture yourself with all the possibilities. You must trust. You must trust that God did what was best for your good and His glory. You must leave it in His hands.

Sometimes you feel guilty for beginning to feel normal and happy again. The first time you laugh you are shocked. You stop yourself. You feel it is a betrayal to move on. You feel you have betrayed the one who is gone because you are able to feel happy without them.

Guilt is a feeling you must put aside. Life moves on and so must you at some point. Your loved one would not want you to mourn forever. They would be broken-hearted to think you could not go on to be happy ever again.

Moving on does not mean you forget. It doesn't mean you don't still love them or won't remember them forever. It just means there are other things in your life that have value and meaning which deserve your attention and your devotion. One does not rule out the other. You can still love the departed one while devoting yourself to the task God has left you behind to accomplish. It's okay to be happy again. It's okay to allow God to heal your heart.

But don't be surprised if you still have periods of mourning at unexpected times when you think you have moved on. A smell or sound can bring back the grief so that it feels as fresh as the day it happened. Holidays, birthdays, and other special days can be very difficult for a very long time. That is normal. But don't let a temporary pain become a permanent set back. Have a good cry and then get on with your life.

Other Storms

Maybe your storm does not involve the loss of a loved one. Maybe you had a financial, emotional, or even personal physical storm. There is still damage control that must be done. You may also need a time of grieving over a loss that is associated with your storm.

You may have lost an ability to do something that was important to you. You may have lost the means to have the financial freedom you once had. You may have lost any number of things. You will probably need a time of grieving over your loss. You may need a time of adjustment to your new way of life.

The Passing of the Storm

When your storm passes, if there is clean up to be done, it is good for you to have a time to grieve your losses too. Then allow God to heal your pains and woes.

Perhaps you are facing a storm that will never pass, at least not here on earth. You know that by all indications you must continue on with the person or thing that has caused such upheaval in your life.

In that case, you may need to grieve the loss of what is gone and find a way to heal in the midst of your storm. Only God can help you do that, but I believe He can if you allow Him to. It may only be by the grace of God that you are able to continue on in your storm, day by day, with no end in sight. But God is able to give you that kind of grace.

II Corinthians 9:8 says, *And God is able to make all grace abound toward you; that ye, always having all sufficiency in all things, may abound to every good work.*

II Corinthians 12:9 says, *And he said unto me, My grace is sufficient for thee: for my strength is made perfect in weakness. Most gladly therefore will I rather glory in my infirmities, that the power of Christ may rest upon me.*

I have a dear friend who is a pastor's wife. She has loved serving the Lord side by side with her husband for many years. She was always busy with the Lord's work and it always amazed me to see how much she was able to accomplish.

Because of a severe and ongoing physical problem, she has lost her ability to keep up her normal schedule. She is most often confined to bed and is in quite a bit of pain. Her problems may be lifelong.

While I am sure she has had times of intense grieving for the loss of the ministry she once had, she has gone on to create a new ministry for God that she can conduct from her bedside. She sends e-mails and writes sweet notes of encouragement to those in her church and to others she knows who need an uplifting boost. She always speaks with optimism and joy in her voice when I talk to her on the phone. And she never seems to lose her sense of humor.

I know that she mourns her losses, but she does what she can for the Lord in the place He has allowed her to be. And she has a ministry of true value, though it is not a ministry she would ever have chosen for herself.

No matter what your storm, no matter where you are in the grieving process, I encourage you to look to God to be everything you need. Draw on His grace. Let Him heal and encourage your heart so you can go on, beyond your storm, to bring glory to Him.

All Tears Dried

I can't end this chapter without talking about eternity. It is the place where your loved one has gone. It is the place where you will once again meet. It is the place where all wrongs will be righted. The Lord will wipe away all tears and sadness. No storms will ever bother you again.

Revelation 21:4 says, *And God shall wipe away all tears from their eyes; and there shall be no more death, neither sorrow, nor crying, neither shall there be any more pain: for the former things are passed away.*

Heaven gives us hope. It is a comfort to know that earth is not all there is. If all life had to offer was what we see here and now, then I believe I would feel like those who think life is a cruel joke. But while life has no purpose to the unsaved person, it has tremendous purpose for us. Life is our proving grounds for eternity.

God puts each one of us here on earth for a purpose. He has a master plan and somehow we all fit into that plan. God watches you as you journey through life. He forms and molds you into the person He wants you to become. He allows trials, testings, and temptations in an attempt to make you into the image of Jesus Christ.

When you realize that this life is temporary, then you can also see that God is preparing you for an eternal existence. You do not end when your life on earth does. Earth and the things of earth are not all there is. Your time here is so short. Eternity, of course, goes on forever and ever. Eternity is where you will spend the rest of your existence. Eternity is the place of true importance.

When I was young I did not look forward to Heaven. I wanted to grow up, get married, have children. I wanted to live a bit more. But the older I get, the more I understand the dear old souls who anxiously await the day when they will enter eternity. For that is when everything of true value begins.

That is when we will see our Savior face to face. That is when we will be reunited with those who have gone on before us. That is when we will be able to praise, honor, and serve God as we never have been able to here on earth.

Heaven is beyond our comprehension. It boggles my mind to think about it. But it will be wonderful. I am sure. And He will be wonderful. Finally we will be able to thank and praise our Lord face to face.

The Passing of the Storm

God promises us a storm-free eternity. So the storms we endure here are insignificant compared to the time when no storm will ever again trouble us.

Life is so short. It is a testing ground for eternity. Let's do our best to pass the test. When life's earthly storms come and when they go, let's determine to honor the Lord in all we do and say, so He will be glorified!

> My heart can sing when I pause to remember
> A heartache here is but a stepping stone
> Along a path that's winding always upward,
> This troubled world is not my final home.
>
> *Until Then* by Stuart Hamblin

CALMING YOUR STORM

- Go ahead and grieve. Don't let others shame you for doing what is natural and right. Take the time you need to cry and express your grief.
- Keep your memories and share them with those who care and understand. Talking about your loved one can aid the grieving process and help you begin to heal.
- Don't feel guilty when the healing process does begin. Instead, thank the Lord that you can smile and laugh again. Remember the good times you had with your loved one and let that be a source of joy.
- Give value to your storm. Find a way to honor your loved one. It doesn't have to be anything big or expensive. Just an act of kindness in their name and in the Lord's name will be of value. Pray about what the Lord would want you to do.
- Remember you are not alone. No matter how fierce the storm that rages around you, you are not alone. God never leaves you alone in your trials. Just as the potter watches his prized vessel in the kiln, so the Master Potter watches you as you go through the fire of adversity. Live in such a way that your life will come out of the fire more beautiful and useful for Him.
- Set your sights higher. Remember that Heaven is your final destination. Someday soon you will be there. Make your life and your storm

experiences count for the Lord. That would be the greatest honor you could give to the one you loved. That would be the best way to bring glory to God.

MEMORIZE THESE VERSES

Isaiah 35:10 *And the ransomed of the LORD shall return, and come to Zion with songs and everlasting joy upon their heads: they shall obtain joy and gladness, and sorrow and sighing shall flee away.*

Isaiah 14:3 *And it shall come to pass in the day that the LORD shall give thee rest from thy sorrow.*

Malachi 4:2 *But unto you that fear my name shall the Sun of righteousness arise with healing in his wings.*

Mark 4:37-39 *And there arose a great storm of wind, and the waves beat into the ship, so that it was now full.*

And he was in the hinder part of the ship, asleep on a pillow: and they awake him, and say unto him, Master, carest thou not that we perish?

And he arose, and rebuked the wind, and said unto the sea, Peace, be still. And the wind ceased, and there was a great calm.

The Value of the Storm

THE VALUE OF AFFLICTION

Enquiring minds want to know, "Why on earth has this happened to me? What value is there in this storm?"

Admit it. You want to know why a storm has come into your life. I know, you are sure that every Christian you know would gasp in horror if you asked that question out loud, but you still wonder, don't you?

I did.

I take comfort in the fact that one of the last things Jesus Christ said on the cross, as He died for our sins, was, "My God, my God, why hast thou forsaken me?"

Jesus asked why.

I have often wonder why He asked, "Why?" He knew why He was dying on the cross. He knew why God could not look on sin and therefore was forced to turn His back. He knew all the answers. Yet still He asked, "Why?"

So why did He ask, "Why?" Could it be that even though Jesus is God the Son, these words were spoken to show how completely He identified with our humanness? In our humanness, we often ask, "Why?" And Jesus understands how we feel. He felt the terrible loneliness of separation from God. He felt forsaken. He felt the way we often feel.

Yet, even when He questioned, He did not reject God. He continued to cling to the fact that God was His God. He confidently said, "My God, my God." We can cling to that fact also. In the moments when we feel lonely and perhaps forsaken, in the times when we ask "Why?" we can also know without a doubt that God is still our God.

Psalm 48:14 says, *For this God is our God for ever and ever: he will be our guide even unto death.*

We will never need to experience separation from God because of what Jesus did when He took our sin. He was separated from His Father in our place. Because of Jesus Christ's death, our God will never turn His back on us.

That is the greatest value of the storm Jesus experienced. Because of Jesus' willingness to be separated from God, the fiercest storm will never separate you from your God. Because of Jesus' storm, someday all your storms will be eternally calmed.

I don't think questioning God is the unpardonable sin. God can handle your questions. But I do believe that deep down, on some level, you must come to the point where you give control to God and quit questioning. It may take time to get to that point when you have been blind-sided with a problem or trial, but I believe the only way to victory in the Christian life is to allow God to have His way without demanding an explanation.

So, go ahead, ask "Why?" But know that just as there was great value to Jesus' storm, there is great value to your storm also. Even if you never know what that value is here on earth, you can trust God to be using your storm for your good and His glory.

Psalm 34:19 says, *Many are the afflictions of the righteous: but the LORD delivereth him out of them all.*

BIBLE ANSWERS TO "WHY?"

I do want to address the question of "Why?"

The Bible gives us some answers when we take the time to look. It turns out there are many different reasons why God allows things to happen to a Christian. The Bible has lots to say about afflictions, trials, temptations, problems, and storms. I was amazed at some of the things the Bible said about affliction. It certainly wasn't what I thought I would find when I began my search. Here are some of the things God has to say about why He allows storms to rage in your life.

It all seems to boil down to the fact that even in the "Why?" times of life, God is working for your good and His glory. I have been saying that

The Value of the Storm

all along. And it's not just wishful thinking on my part. Scripture points to the fact that storms are for your good and storms are for God's glory.

Your storms are not senseless and aimless. They are of great value and purpose. God allows storms so you can draw constantly closer to Him, so you can be more effective in your service to Him, so you can help others, and so your life can be a thing of beauty that brings glory to Him.

WHY? FOR YOUR GOOD

Let's look at some of the "Why's" that are for your good.

Why? To draw you near to God.
Psalm 119:67 says, *Before I was afflicted I went astray: but now have I kept thy word.*

We tend to wander away, just like the sheep God so often compares us to in the Bible. Sometimes we wander astray because of sin that tempts and teases us to go places we ought not to go. Sometimes we wander just by lack of attention. Like a sheep that gets so caught up in feeding and looking ahead for greener grazing places, we also get our eyes off our Shepherd and onto things that look interesting and enticing. Off we wander. The next thing we know, because of the sin that distances us from God or the enticements of the World that lure our attention away from Him, we find ourselves far from where we ought to be. We have gone astray.

God knows it is always in our best interest to stay close to Him. He is our place of sustenance and safety. Just as the sheep that has wandered away is in danger of being harmed, so we are in danger from Satan and the World if we stray far from our Shepherd.

So God wants us to draw near.

I would suppose God would prefer it if we were to look up and see how far we have wandered away from Him and say, "My, I need to get back by my Shepherd's side!" But that rarely happens. So in that case, He must cause us to flee back to Him. He must do something to get our attention. That something is usually a storm.

When life is going peachy and skies are blue, then I tend to forget how much I need the care and protection of my Shepherd. Foolish of me, I know, but that is the way I am. But when the storm clouds roll in and the thunder rumbles, I take notice. Then I begin to think, "Hmm, I sure am far away from the One who is my fortress and shield! I had better get back to Him!"

Storms make us look up and help us to see how far we have wandered away from God. That is for our good. A storm may be the only thing that causes us to go running back into His arms and desire to stay close for shelter.

So, when a storm looms on your horizon, take a moment to think, "Am I close to my God? Have I gone astray? Could this be God's way of drawing me close to Him?" If you find that is the case, then run, don't walk, back to the Lord!

Psalm 73:28 says, *But it is good for me to draw near to God: I have put my trust in the Lord GOD, that I may declare all thy works.*

James 4:8 says, *Draw nigh to God, and he will draw nigh to you. Cleanse your hands, ye sinners; and purify your hearts, ye double minded.*

Why? To strengthen you.
God wants you to be strong in your Christian life.

You have heard the saying, "That which does not kill you makes you stronger." There is truth in that. Trials, testings, and afflictions all cause you to grow stronger. They make you exercise your faith muscles.

I Peter 5:8-10 says, *Be sober, be vigilant; because your adversary the devil, as a roaring lion, walketh about, seeking whom he may devour:*

Whom resist stedfast in the faith, knowing that the same afflictions are accomplished in your brethren that are in the world.

But the God of all grace, who hath called us unto his eternal glory by Christ Jesus, after that ye have suffered a while, make you perfect, stablish, strengthen, settle you.

In order to become strong, you must be a courageous soldier of God. As we talked about in the chapter on courage, if you put forth the effort to have courage, God will always be right there to back you up. If you do your part to resist Satan and the trials he throws your way, God will make you "perfect, stablish, strengthen, settle you."

While you are in this world, you not only have storms to contend with, you also have an enemy who would dearly love to see you destroyed. But Satan cannot destroy you when you stay close to God and you are equipped with the strength God gives to you. It is only when you are far from God and too weak to resist that Satan can gain a victory over you. That never needs to happen.

The Value of the Storm

I John 4:4 tells us, *Ye are of God, little children, and have overcome them: because greater is he that is in you, than he that is in the world.*

Who is the "them" that you have overcome through God? Satan, the World, and your own sinful flesh. God can give you strength to overcome them all. The storms in your life can build your faith muscles and give you the strength to do just that.

Why? To teach you to be more Christ-Like.

God actually said that affliction is good for us. Good?

Psalm 119:71 says, *It is good for me that I have been afflicted; that I might learn thy statutes.*

Hmm. I have never thought of problems as being good. They are something that can be endured if I must. They are something that can bring about good. But to say a problem is good? That was something I would never naturally do. But God said problems can be good.

So what's the good part? The good part is that afflictions cause you to go to God's Word. It is there you can learn to be more like Christ.

Psalm 119:75 tells us, *I know, O LORD, that thy judgments are right, and that thou in faithfulness hast afflicted me.*

Psalm 119:92 says, *Unless thy law had been my delights, I should then have perished in mine affliction.*

God wants you to be more Christ-like. He wants you to learn things that will make you stronger and more mature in your Christian walk. The only way you will become more Christ-like here on earth is for you to learn the lessons that can only be learned from God's Word.

God's statutes and judgements teach us many valuable lessons. In fact, everything we know of God and of how to reach Him and serve Him is found in His Word alone. There is nowhere else to go to learn about God. So daily we should be searching God's Statutes so we can be learning.

But we often don't like to learn the lessons God's Word has to teach us. We might prefer to pick and choose from God's Word. If the lesson suits us, then we accept it. If it doesn't suit us and our way of living, then we ignore it.

When we ignore the lessons God has to teach us, because He loves us, He has to get our attention. He sends afflictions to open our eyes and make us willing to learn.

My mother always loved to tell the story of my first day at kindergarten. I was all of four years old and I had previously been attending a preschool that was held in our church's basement. I loved preschool. We spent the entire morning finger painting and playing. Then afterwards I would go next door to stay with the Pastor's wife until my mom came to pick me up. The Pastor's wife was a kind lady who fixed me peanut butter sandwiches just the way I loved them. They were the "Peanuttiest!" Preschool was the best!

Then came the day when I had to go to "real" school. From the beginning, I just knew it wasn't going to be a pleasant experience. It scared me. I had to ride a bus for a couple of blocks to reach the school. I remember the bus looked big and intimidating. I was adamant about not getting on the bus. Finally the bus driver suggested that my mom could ride along on the way to school.

I don't remember much about the first day of school, but my mother says when I stepped off the bus after school I began to cry. Mom knelt in front of me and asked what was wrong. Between sobs I choked out the problem. I dramatically informed her why I didn't like school.

"They want me to learn, and I don't want to learn!" I exclaimed with a glare and a pout. My finger painting days were over and I was one very unhappy little girl.

Well, I often think I haven't gotten too far beyond that attitude about many things in my life. Many times when God has a lesson He wants to teach me, I still find myself going to Him and sobbing, "God, you want me to learn, and I don't want to learn!"

It can be hard to learn certain lessons in life. Why? Because learning new lessons usually involves a thing we all tend to distrust and avoid. It's called CHANGE.

You see, when we discover something shouldn't be in our life, or we learn how something needs to be done, then usually a change must occur for that to come about. And people hate change. It totally disrupts life as we know it. Change can cause some very big storms. But change is necessary if we ever hope to become more like Christ.

In our sinful condition we are nothing like Christ. In fact, we start out the total opposite of what Christ is like. When we get saved, that's the first step, but it's only the first step. We have to make lots of changes to become more and more like Him. Yet we often resist.

Over the years I have tried to learn to be teachable. I have tried to remember that change isn't always bad. In fact, if it's a change God wants to make in my life, then the change will always be for my good. The change will make me more Christ-like.

That is the goal that is set before each of us. So, yes, a storm that teaches us a lesson we need to learn is good for us. It is good because it causes us to be more like Christ.

Romans 8:28-29a says, *And we know that all things work together for good to them that love God, to them who are the called according to his purpose.*

For whom he did foreknow, he also did predestinate to be conformed to the image of his Son.

WHY? FOR HIS GLORY

Now let's look at some of the why's that are for God's glory.

Why? To help you reach out to others.

In the early 1980's I was a student at Bob Jones University. One day, as I prepared for my exams, I received a phone call from my father. He was calling to tell me Mom had breast cancer. She had been immediately admitted to the hospital and they were planning surgery for the next day. Dad said, "Don't come home. Not yet. Everything may turn out fine. You can come home later if you need to. Stay and take your exams."

Needless to say, it was very hard to concentrate. I didn't realize it, but I must have been walking around campus with a long face because one of my teachers spotted me in the hallway the next day and pulled me aside.

"What's wrong, Wendy?" she asked. I briefly explained what was happening with my mom.

"Do you have a few minutes to come to my office now?" I did. So we sat down and I poured my heart out to her. All my worries and concerns tumbled out. After she listened, she offered a few words of encouragement. Then she prayed for me.

She didn't solve any of my problems, but my heart felt lighter. My faith was stronger. Just knowing someone else cared enough to listen and to pray made a big difference. It lightened my load.

God intends that we should be ready to reach out a helping hand to others who are in need.

II Corinthians 1:3-4 says, *Blessed be God, even the Father of our Lord Jesus Christ, the Father of mercies, and the God of all comfort;*

Who comforteth us in all our tribulation, that we may be able to comfort them which are in any trouble, by the comfort wherewith we ourselves are comforted of God.

God so freely offers His comfort to us. A Christ-like gesture that brings glory to God is to turn to others and offer our comfort just as God offered comfort to us in our time of need.

It isn't hard to offer God's comfort to others. Just a listening ear, a word of encouragement, and a prayer can make all the difference to someone. For a Christian, it can encourage them and give them the strength to keep on trusting the Lord through their storm. For an unsaved person, it can be a wonderful opportunity to witness for the Lord and share how God can be there to help them. It can mean the salvation of their soul.

So, if you have ever been offered a helping hand when you were in need, don't forget to turn around and reach out your hand to someone else who is in need. In doing so, you will bring glory to God.

Why? To help you give praise to God.

The following verses from Psalm 107 paint a vivid picture of a ship at sea that is being tossed about by a mighty storm. As the men aboard stagger about on the ship, because of the great waves that threaten them, the Scripture says when they cry to God, He hears and delivers. God's deliverance certainly is cause for bringing praise and glory to God.

Psalm 107:25-31 says, *For he commandeth, and raiseth the stormy wind, which lifteth up the waves thereof.*

They mount up to the heaven, they go down again to the depths: their soul is melted because of trouble.

They reel to and fro, and stagger like a drunken man, and are at their wits' end.

Then they cry unto the LORD in their trouble, and he bringeth them out of their distresses.

He maketh the storm a calm, so that the waves thereof are still.

Then are they glad because they be quiet; so he bringeth them unto their desired haven.

Oh that men would praise the LORD for his goodness, and for his wonderful works to the children of men!

The Value of the Storm

Sounds like the storms of life that toss us about at times. We must call on the Lord and He will deliver us, in His time and in His way. We need to remember to praise Him for His goodness to us.

Sometimes we are tossed about on life's sea as a means of testing our faith. If we can remain faithful and continue to praise Him, even while the storm is at it's worst, that brings glory to God. Others will see that we can praise Him even before we have been rescued from the storm. Our faith and trust in God brings glory to His name.

God deserves our glory and praise. Praise to God should be continually on our lips. He longs to hear our praise in His ears. But often, when the seas of life are calm, we forget to offer praise to Him. Many times it takes a storm to turn us to Him and when He delivers us, then we remember to praise Him.

I Peter 1:6-7 says, *Wherein ye greatly rejoice, though now for a season, if need be, ye are in heaviness through manifold temptations:*

That the trial of your faith, being much more precious than of gold that perisheth, though it be tried with fire, might be found unto praise and honour and glory at the appearing of Jesus Christ.

I don't know why God tests our faith. It seems He does test His children. He tested Abraham to see if he was willing to offer his only son Isaac. God tested Job. Or rather, He allowed Satan to test Job. Most likely, Job didn't know until he got to Heaven the reason for his testings. He didn't know there was a spiritual battle taking place. But Job stayed faithful to God and God received the glory because of it.

Perhaps God is testing you. Make sure you go to Him in your time of trouble. And make sure you remember to offer Him the glory and praise He deserves. Not just when the storm has ended, but in the midst of your storm give Him the glory that is His.

Isaiah 48:10-11 says, *Behold, I have refined thee, but not with silver; I have chosen thee in the furnace of affliction.*

For mine own sake, even for mine own sake, will I do it: for how should my name be polluted? and I will not give my glory unto another.

Psalm 40:3 says, *And he hath put a new song in my mouth, even praise unto our God: many shall see it, and fear, and shall trust in the LORD.*

If we can offer praise to God, even during times of trial and testing, it brings glory to His name. Who better to bring glory to God then His own children? What a sweet sacrifice we offer to Him when we give Him praise in the midst of our storm!

Psalm 107:31 *Oh that men would praise the LORD for his goodness, and for his wonderful works to the children of men!*

Lessons From The Storm

There is purpose and value in every storm you weather. You may not always see it immediately. In fact, you may not see it until you reach eternity. But whether or not you are able to determine the purpose and value of a storm at the present time, you can learn many valuable lessons that will aid you here on earth.

In my storms I have learned so much about God but I have also learned quite a bit about myself too. I wasn't too surprised I had a lot to learn about God, but I was quite surprised there was so much I didn't know about my own heart and mind.

God knows me inside and out and He wants me to learn more about my thoughts, feelings, motives, and actions so that everything I do and say will be according to His will. He wants me to learn about the thoughts and intents of my heart so I can make the corrections needed to be more Christ-like.

Often God uses a storm to teach us those valuable life lessons. So let me share a few of the lessons I have learned in my storms. You may learn entirely different lessons because you are an entirely different person and your storms will be entirely different from mine, but maybe some of what I have learned will also apply to you.

Trials bring out the real me.

I can be pretty good about showing others the side of me I want them to see, but when a storm comes along all pretense slips away. I begin to think and speak and act from the depths of who I am. I am not always pleased with what I find deep inside myself that comes spilling out.

I have a cowlick on the back of my head. In the morning I style my hair and from my perspective in the front it looks pretty good. But often, when I take a mirror and look at the back of my head, I see where my cowlick has left an open spot. I am quick to correct it with comb and hair spray. Without the mirror I would never have seen the problem. Without a mirror to show me a different perspective it would never be fixed.

God can see me inside and out. No mask can fool Him. He knows

The Value of the Storm

my every flaw. He sees what I cannot see. He knows things about me that I do not know or am not willing to face about myself.

When a storm dredges up uncertainty, fear, unkind words, and angry feelings, I am ashamed of myself. It is as if God holds up a mirror and allows me to see what I could not or would not see before.

If I am wise, I will see that God is using a storm to hold a mirror up for me to examine what I could not see from my normal perspective. I will see this eye-opening experience as an opportunity to rid my life of the ugly sins that weigh me down spiritually. I will make the changes needed so I will be more Christ-like, inside and out.

God wants you to be a person who is totally obedient and yielded to Him. He wants the real you to be Christ-like. He uses His Word to show you your heart. He may also use a storm as a mirror to show you parts of yourself that you could not see from the perspective of a calm life. It may take a storm to bring out the real you. It may take a storm to show you what is truly inside.

Don't close your eyes and ignore the ugly things you see. Instead, use that eye-opening opportunity to make the changes needed to cause your life to be more beautiful and more Christ-like.

Prayer changes me.

We have all heard the saying, "Prayer changes things." I don't really like that saying. It is a very limited way to look at prayer. I also think it is a selfish way of looking at our communication with God. It makes it sound like God is a magic genie who does all we request if we just take the time to tell Him what we want and when we want it.

I don't think that is the purpose of prayer at all. Prayer is not just a request or demand time when the most powerful One in the universe checks in with us to see how we think things should be done.

God knows what is best for us. He does what is best for us. If God does grant your petitions, then maybe it is the best thing for you, but it may also be that you have demanded in such a way that God decides to give you your way and let you live with the consequences. That doesn't sound like something I would want. I don't want God to do something just because I have decided it is what I think should be done. I don't want my own selfish way when God's way is always so much better.

Prayer should be about God, not you and your desires. It should be about conforming to God's will and growing closer to Him.

When we are in a storm our inclination is to pray for relief or to pray for a desired outcome. It is hard to say, "God, I want You to have Your way in this situation. Do what You think is best." Especially when you know what God thinks is best may be something difficult and painful for you.

I began to realize many years ago that prayer was really a time when I could get alone with God and tell Him what was on my heart. True, it often includes my problems and what I think would be a nice outcome, but I have learned God's outcomes are much better than anything I could ask for.

I also began to realize my prayer time is an opportunity for God to speak to me. I now see prayer as a two-way communication. I speak to God and He speaks to my heart. He molds my desires. He prepares my heart for what He has planned. He gives comfort and peace by His presence.

Prayer helps me to get in tune with God. It makes me feel close to Him. And the closer I get to God, the more I am willing to accept His will for my life. The closer I get to God, the more I desire His will for my life because I realize God is so good and He only wants what is best in the grand scheme of things.

Often I have begun to pray about something that distresses me. I think I know how I want God to work things out, but as I draw close, He begins to change my heart. I begin to see things from a different perspective. I become more pliable to His will. I desire to yield to Him. And when He takes the situation I am praying about in a different direction from what I expected, I can trust Him to be doing what is best.

So I have learned prayer does not always change things, but it always, if I allow it, changes me. And anytime God changes me, He is changing me to become more Christ-like. That is of true value.

Change Me

Dear Lord, change not Thy will in my life,
Or trial and sorrows to be;
Renew my faith and make me strong,
Change not Thy will, change me.

Though teardrops fall when trouble comes,
Like storms on a rolling sea;
Let Thy beacon guide my ship to port,
Change not the storm, change me.

The Value of the Storm

When Thy Holy Word I don't understand
And Thy glory I cannot see;
Teach my eyes, give me sight and wisdom,
Change not Thy Word, change me.

If the fruit Thou hast given me to eat,
Taste bitter and sour, I plea;
Let not my will but Thine be done,
Change not the fruit, change me.

If sometime I murmur and grumble, dear Lord,
About the cross I carry for Thee;
Keep it firm on my shoulders, but hold my hand,
Change not the cross, change me.

If You change Thy ways to please me, dear Lord,
I would soon grow cold and turn from Thee;
That You may hear my prayers, dear Lord,
Change not Thy ways, change me.

There's a valley that I must cross,
Someday Thy face to see;
Lest I forget what power is Thine,
Change not the valley, change me.

Author Unknown

I never face a storm alone.

I have felt very alone in some of my storms. Sometimes it seemed no one understood or even if they did, they couldn't help. That was discouraging and frightening. But in the middle of my storm, God has clearly shown me I am not alone. No matter how fierce the storm rages or how long it lasts, He is right there beside me.

Gary throws pottery and he often takes his wheel and some clay to churches to do a demonstration. He talks about God, the Master Potter, and us, the clay. It is amazing how closely the process of making a piece of pottery parallels our Christian lives.

At one point Gary talks about how the pottery must go through the fire, not to destroy the piece, but to make it into a useful vessel. When the potter places the pot into the fire, he does not turn on the heat and walk away. He does not leave the clay alone in the fire. Instead, he watches closely through the "eye." He watches the progress and never lets the piece be fired above what it is able to handle.

God is the Master Potter. When He allows you to go through the fire, He is right there with you. He watches carefully. He knows exactly what you can take. He allows the fire in your life so that when you come out, you will be a useful vessel for Him.

You are never alone in the fire. God is there with you. What a comfort to know that the fire will not consume you. It will only refine you and make you into a servant who is pleasing and of great value to Him.

God is always near. Just knowing you don't face the storm alone and that God has a purpose for the storm can help so much. It gives you something solid to which you can cling. It gives value and purpose to everything. It helps you to redeem the pain and suffering.

Hebrews 13:5b says, *I will never leave thee, nor forsake thee.*

Isaiah 43:1b-2, 4a says, *Fear not: for I have redeemed thee, I have called thee by thy name; thou art mine.*

When thou passest through the waters, I will be with thee; and through the rivers, they shall not overflow thee: when thou walkest through the fire, thou shalt not be burned; neither shall the flame kindle upon thee.

Since thou wast precious in my sight.

It's not easy to be Christ-Like, but it's worthwhile.

The struggle to be Christ-like is ongoing. The battle is minute by minute. It doesn't matter whether you are in a storm or whether your life is calm. Satan, your old nature, and the World fight daily to defeat you and your testimony.

This is one struggle you must not weary of. You must keep fighting. You must be vigilant and aware. You must be ready to ward off the enemy, regardless of whether it is an enemy from without or from within.

The good news is that you do not fight alone. God waits to give deliverance when you cry to Him. Jesus Christ is constantly standing before the throne of grace interceding for you. And the Holy Spirit dwells within you to help you each step of the way. You cannot have stronger allies than these. They provide all you need to daily win your battles.

The Value of the Storm

They continually encourage you, help you, and give you the strength and wisdom to do what you should. They constantly work to help you to be more Christ-like. You only need to listen and obey.

I was about four years old when I first went with my mother to her China painting classes. I remember playing on the floor under the big table where five or six women sat with paint and brushes and china plates learning to paint. The teacher would walk from student to student to give advice and instruction.

Eventually Mom learned enough that she could paint without a teacher's help. She bought all the supplies she needed and lots of plain china bowls, plates, and vases. She bought a kiln to fire her dishes.

For years Mom did china painting. Everyday when I got home from school, there would be Mom, sitting at a small table in the living room that was piled high with all the necessary equipment to paint china.

The dishes were beautiful. Mother painted roses, and little birds, and acorns with autumn leaves. But the thing Mom loved to paint most was pansies. Pansies were Mom's favorite flower.

As I grew older, I began to realize how much time, effort, and talent went into painting a dish. I would watch as Mom would start out with a plain china dish. It was pure white and shiny without a single mark on it. It could have been used just as it was, but by the time Mom got done with it, many weeks later, the dish would be so much more special.

Mom would start by taking a wax pencil and lightly sketching the outline of several pansies and their stems and leaves onto the plain plate. Next she would mix oil and powdered paint colors on a palette and dip her brush into the paint. Sometimes she would mix two colors together to get the exact shade she desired.

Then she began to paint. At first, the plate didn't look like much. Mom would only paint the outline of the flowers on the dish. Then she would place the plate into the kiln. For hours the kiln would heat. I wasn't allowed too near the kiln because it got extremely hot, but occasionally Mom would allow me a peek inside.

There was a hole on the side of the kiln called the "eye." Mom could remove the piece of brick that covered the eye and look inside the kiln while it was heating. Everything inside was glowing red hot. Mom would look at a small cone she had placed near the eye. When the cone melted, it was time to turn off the kiln and let the plate cool down.

The next day, after the dish was completely cool, Mom would remove it from the kiln and begin to paint on the plate again. This time she would add a bit more detail. The stems would be darkened a bit. The petals of the pansies would be given more color. Then back into the kiln the dish would go.

Again the process of firing the dish in the red hot kiln would be repeated.

The next day, when the dish had again cooled, Mom would again add more paint. Each stroke of the brush added more detail, causing the pansies to look more and more like real flowers.

Into the kiln the dish would go again and again. This process went on and on. After the flowers looked complete, I was sure the dish was done. But Mom would add background shading to give the piece depth. Then back to the fire it went. The final step would be a rim of gold paint around the edge. And one last firing.

What amazing patience and attention to detail a single plate took in order for it to be completed. But Mom knew exactly what was needed to make that plate beautiful.

The plate could have been used before a single drop of paint had been applied, but how plain and drab the plate would have been. After each firing, the plate could have been used. But with each new detail that was added, the plate became more and more beautiful.

The dishes Mom painted will be treasured for as long as I own them. I display many of Mother's dishes in my kitchen and their beauty will be admired for years to come. They have great value to me, especially since I remember how much time and effort went into each dish.

Did you know your life is a bit like a plain china plate? God is the master artist. In His mind he knows exactly what He wants to make of your life. He wants your life to be a thing of beauty that will bring glory and honor to Him. With great care God adds detail after detail. He knows exactly what needs to be applied to our lives to make us like He wants us.

Again and again we are placed in the furnace of affliction. But always, if we allow Him, God uses the affliction to add depth and beauty to our lives. Each new affliction adds value.

Do you know, not once did a plate turn to my mom and say, "What? Pansies again? I wanted to be painted with roses instead!" Sometimes when God begins to add the details to our lives, we turn to God and say,

The Value of the Storm

"No, God. I don't want to do that. I think you have made a mistake with my life."

Unlike a plate which has absolutely no say in what will be done with it, we turn to God and tell Him we don't want to do things His way. But God is all-knowing. He knows what is best for us. He knows what He wants to make of us. He knows what is needed to make us into His image.

Never did a plate turn to my mom and say, "I've had enough of this. Can't you work faster?" At times we may feel like the process of shaping our life is never ending. We often balk at God and wish the process was ended. It may seem to take a long time to be fashioned into what God intends us to be, yet in God's perfect time we are being made into the exact vessel God has in mind.

With each new stroke of His brush, if you allow Him, your life becomes more and more beautiful for Him. With each stroke, your life becomes more Christ-like. It will be a thing of lasting beauty and value, not just for here on earth, but for all eternity.

Are you allowing God to work in your life? Are you becoming more Christ-like each day?

Satisfied

All of the above may not answer the "Why's" of your specific storm, but I have found that knowing the answer does not always bring comfort. Knowing why doesn't always make your storm seem any more fair. Answers may make you wiser, but rarely do they make the storm any more pleasant to bear.

Here on earth you may never have all the answers because you are unable to see the big picture of what God is truly doing. Let me assure you, someday all the "Why's" will be answered. All wrongs will be righted. Until that day, I suggest that you determine to focus with eyes of faith on the Christ who loves you. Rest in Him to do what is best for your good and His glory. Then, when you see Him face to face, you will know why and you will be completely satisfied.

There Is Light At The End Of The Tunnel

The old saying goes, "There's a light at the end of the tunnel." We've also heard the sarcastic comeback, "Yeah, there's a light at the end of the tunnel and it's a train!"

This week in the newspaper the Ziggy cartoon showed Ziggy talking with someone. His nose was all bandaged up. He was explaining, "I got burned by the light at the end of the tunnel."

Amusing, but both Ziggy and the old saying are wrong. There is a light at the end of your tunnel, but that light is Jesus Christ and the eternity He offers to you in Heaven. Trust helps us to believe there is hope, even in the worst storm. Jesus Christ is truly the light at the end of our tunnel. Heaven is where we will find Him. No storm will ever again disturb us when we get there.

I love the passage in Revelation that talks about Heaven. Let me skip around a bit as you read several verses from Revelation 21.

Revelation 21:1,4,10,18,22-23 says, *And I saw a new heaven and a new earth: for the first heaven and the first earth were passed away; and there was no more sea.*

And God shall wipe away all tears from their eyes: and there shall be no more death, neither sorrow, nor crying, neither shall there be any more pain: for the former things are passed away.

And he carried me away in the spirit to a great and high mountain, and shewed me that great city, the holy Jerusalem, descending out of heaven from God.

And the building of the wall of it was of jasper: and the city was pure gold, like unto clear glass.

And I saw no temple therein: for the Lord God Almighty and the Lamb are the temple of it.

And the city had no need of the sun, neither of the moon, to shine in it: for the glory of God did lighten it, and the Lamb is the light thereof.

While we go through a storm in life, it seems never ending and all-consuming. But there will be an end to it someday. Even if we have to endure a storm that lasts a lifetime here on earth, one day all storms will pass away for good. Jesus Christ, the Lamb of God, is the light at the end of the tunnel. He is the calm that awaits us in Heaven.

The Value of the Storm

When we get to heaven all will be perfect calm. We will never again experience pain, sorrow, or death. We will never again have to say goodbye to ones we love. Our old sinful nature will no longer trouble us. We will live with the One who loves us with a perfect love. We will serve Him perfectly. We will be with Him forever. We will finally be Christ-like in every way.

In Heaven, all of life's trials will be explained. Life's storms will end, never to return. But I imagine that when we get there, we won't care about the "whys" anymore. Instead I think we will turn our once tearful gazes away from the past and, with hearts filled with joy, we will be totally focused on worshipping and serving our Lord. Our peace will be perfect. Calm will reign.

Finally and forever, all storms will be banished.

CALMING YOUR STORM

- Explore the "Why's" in the Scripture. See how God wants to do what is best for you by drawing you close, by strengthening you, and by making you more Christ-like.
- See how God wants your life to bring glory to Him by helping others and by praising Him. Put what you discover into practice.
- Ask God to let you know what lessons you need to learn from your storms. Search the Scriptures. Ponder the lessons you learn. Then find everyday, practical ways to put those lessons to work in your life.
- When trials bring out the real you, instead of turning a blind eye away from the mirror God holds up, be brave enough to take a look. Then ask God to help you make the changes necessary to make your life pleasing to Him.
- Take a close look at your prayer life. Does your prayer list read like a wish list out of a Sears catalog? Are you treating God like a magic genie? Make some adjustments. Make prayer a time when you not only go to God with your requests, but also a time when you allow God to speak to your heart. Be yielded to the changes He wants to make in your life.
- Remember that you never face your storms alone. Draw courage and strength from His presence.
- Ask God to help you to be teachable. Ask Him to prepare your heart to make changes that will cause you to be more Christ-like.

• Spend some time praising God for the things He is doing in your life through the storm. Praise Him that this stormy life is not all that you have to look forward to. Instead, rejoice because Heaven and an eternity with God is yours!

Memorize These Verses

Psalm 34:19 *Many are the afflictions of the righteous: but the LORD delivereth him out of them all.*

I Peter 1:6-7 *Wherein ye greatly rejoice, though now for a season, if need be, ye are in heaviness through manifold temptations:*

That the trial of your faith, being much more precious than of gold that perisheth, though it be tried with fire, might be found unto praise and honour and glory at the appearing of Jesus Christ.

Psalm 119:92 *Unless thy law had been my delights, I should then have perished in mine affliction.*

Psalm 107:31 *Oh that men would praise the LORD for his goodness, and for his wonderful works to the children of men!*

Made in the USA
Columbia, SC
01 May 2018